THE

PRINCIPLES OF CRITICISM

THE PRINCIPLES OF CRITICISM

CRITICISM

AN INTRODUCTION TO THE STUDY OF LITERATURE

BY

W. BASIL WORSFOLD, M.A.

KENNIKAT PRESS
Port Washington, N. Y./London

THE PRINCIPLES OF CRITICISM

First published in 1902
Reissued in 1970 by Kennikat Press
Library of Congress Catalog Card No: 75-105857
ISBN 0-8046-0991-8

Manufactured by Taylor Publishing Company   Dallas, Texas

TO THE READER

THE purpose of this book is to present an account of the main principles of literary criticism, and to illustrate these principles by passages from great writers.

The book will, therefore, be found to contain (in addition to the text) a collection of noteworthy critical utterances.

The translations from the Greek, German, and French have been done by the Author.

References are made (with two exceptions) to the text of Aristotle by the pages of Immanuel Bekker's large (Berlin) edition; and to that of Plato, by the pages of the edition of Henry Stephens. Addison is cited by numbers of the Spectator, *and Lessing by chapters of the* Laocoon. *In the case of other authors, the footnotes will sufficiently indicate the sources of reference.*

Both an index of authors and an index of subjects have been provided.

W. B. W.

RIDGE, NEAR CAPEL, SURREY,
November 1, 1902.

TABLE OF CONTENTS

THE PRINCIPLES OF CRITICISM

INTRODUCTORY

I. ASPECTS OF LITERATURE

I SUPPOSE that it will not be denied that comparison lies at the root of all our judgments in art and literature, and that our judgments are valid in proportion as the range of experience on which they are based is of greater or less extent. It is the principle in which Burke finds a foundation for the belief in the existence of a general standard of taste. A man who has never seen a piece of sculpture admires the representations of the human head afforded by a barber's shop; but his admiration for the waxen effigies of the barber is killed by a visit to a studio. The ordinary processes which minister to mental growth and to the training of eye and ear—education, experience, travel, and opportunities of social converse—together provide material which, unconsciously applied, is sufficient to enable us to form approximately correct judgments on every-day questions. In this way we become sensible to the charm of painting and music, learn to distinguish between a harmonious and an inharmonious arrangement of form and colour, and are quickly affected by any sense of incongruity in our social or material surroundings.

For all the purposes of every-day life taste will serve.

But if we go round a picture gallery with an artist we soon find that while 'taste' makes the sight of these pictures a genuine enjoyment, it will go only a little way towards helping us to discriminate between the relative merits of the several works. Broadly speaking, we do not see much difference in them. But the artist, or the critic, sees both the excellences and defects to which our eyes are blind.

As with art, so with literature. We read this or that book because, as we say, it 'interests' us, or it 'amuses' us. Our taste leads us to prefer one book to another, or one branch of literature, or style of writing, to another ; but it does not enable us to explain the grounds on which in each case our preferences are based. Some readers do not care to analyse their feelings. For them this book will have little or no interest. But there are others—and they form an increasingly large proportion of the entire mass of readers of books—who have passed beyond the stage of unconscious pleasure, and who wish not merely to *read* but to *study* books. For them this book may have an interest, because the study of any form of literature cannot be usefully undertaken without a certain basis of independent knowledge. Inasmuch as literature in its higher forms is an art, the student of literature must be also a critic of literature. As he proceeds in his reading and acquires experience, he will, consciously or unconsciously, assume this attitude. He will not be satisfied with saying, 'This pleases me'; but he will also ask, 'Why does it please me ?' and 'Ought it to please me ?' If these questions are to be answered, the reader must be able to take up a point of view outside the particular work upon which he is engaged.

The main purpose of this book is to supply such an independent point of view : a point of view from which not merely a single period, or a single author, can be approached, but one from which all literature, as literature, can be looked upon. In it I have endeavoured to lay before the reader materials which will enable him to see how some great critics, ancient and modern, have approached the consideration of literature. And here I desire to say a word upon the choice of the authors selected. I do not suggest for a moment that the selection which I have made is the best possible, still less that it is complete ; but I think that the principle which has guided me in making it is one which will be recognised as intelligible. I have endeavoured to select such critics, or such parts of the works of critical writers, as deal with literature as a whole. That is to say, the inquiries which are here brought together are inquiries which deal primarily with principles of criticism, and, only in a secondary degree, with the application of those principles to the examination of particular works. At the same time, in the analyses and extracts which I have placed before the reader, I have endeavoured to indicate the relationship of one method to another, and to some extent to harmonise the different points of view from which master minds have regarded literature. Indeed, one conspicuous result of the comparison afforded by these pages will, I trust, be to establish the fact that validity of judgment is not to be assigned to any single test ; but that a work of literature must often be approached from more than one side, and that a true account of its merits or deficiencies can only be given by applying several tests, and these tests in degrees which vary with the character of the given work.

In the case of one book it may be best to apply the test of truth, and ask with Plato, 'Is the body of information which this book conveys consistent with the facts of life?' In the case of another it may be best to apply the test of symmetry, and ask with Aristotle, 'Is this work constructed in the best possible manner, having regard both to the form of literature to which it belongs, and the common purpose of art, which is to give pleasure?' And, moreover, if we adopt the former of these two central principles, we shall find that we must go further than Plato takes us ; for we must distinguish between the truth of art and the truth of logic. In the case of a work of poetry and of prose-fiction we require a more subtle test. We must ask, 'Does it convey not merely truth as being consistent with the facts of life, but truth as consistent with the mental rendering of those facts—the general conceptions that are based not upon the here and now of every-day experience, but on the generalised experience of more than one country and of more than one age?' That is the truth of art. And because such truth can only be attained by minds that unite a wide range of experience with a resolute determination to know the best, Matthew Arnold finds the 'high seriousness of absolute sincerity,' to be the test of the highest order of poetic merit. When the poet and the artist embody this wider purview in their works—*idealize*, in a word—poetry, by virtue of the contrast between this ideal rendering of the facts of life, and these facts as they are presented to us in every-day experience, becomes a 'criticism' of life, and art a 'criticism' of nature.

Similarly, in adopting the artistic standpoint and in applying the test of symmetry, we have to notice that the symmetry required of each art, and of each form of the several arts, is different. 'Symmetry,' from this closer standpoint, becomes 'composition'; for constructive excellence is resolved into an adaptation of the special means of the special art to the particular purpose which it seeks to fulfil. And in order to judge of this excellence—excellence of *technique*—we must have a knowledge of these means. Here the analyses of the processes of literary and artistic production given by Lessing and Victor Cousin, and their inquiries into the limits of the several arts, provide us with at least the 'bare necessaries' for judgments based upon such artistic considerations.

Let me give an example of a critical difficulty which arises solely from the neglect to discriminate between the different purposes of different forms of literature. Popular judgment is in favour of a 'happy ending' in a novel, but it is commonly maintained that such a termination of the plot is at variance with the canons of criticism, because Aristotle (and other critics after him) has declared the plot ending in 'disaster' to be the most effective and the most artistic. As a matter of fact, the plot terminating in a disaster is required for the one form of literature, the tragedy, where intense pathos, the appeal to the emotions of fear and pity, is the central effect sought to be produced. But in the case of novels in general the principle of 'poetic justice' applies; since only a small class depend entirely, or mainly, upon pathos for their effect. In other words, the 'disaster' is essential to the tragedy, but only incidental to the novel. In prose-fiction, as the vehicle which gives the widest and most varied picture of life, the natural tendency of the human mind towards optimism coincides with the idealizing process of art, and we are justified on both philosophic and critical grounds in expecting to find in prose-fiction 'a more exact goodness and a more absolute variety than can be found in the nature of things.'[1]

Once more to take a third standpoint. The enlarged psychological knowledge which modern science has put at our disposal, and the expanded range of the imagination due to the quickening of the pulse of life by modern inventions, and by the increased and increasing facilities of inter-communication, together form a notable feature in the progress of man. In view of this, Addison's proposal to measure literature by the degree in which it possesses the power to affect the imagination, acquires a new significance. For here we have a test which is applicable to every species of literature, and one which measures a work of literature by reference to what experience now shows to be a merit of increasing importance. It is only by the application of this test that the experience of the booksellers can be harmonized with our belief in the validity of critical principles. By the application of this test we can discern merit in works of literature, which, being entirely defective on the side of construction, yield no reply to any test of formal or artistic canons. Defective in all else, they have yet this one virtue of stimulating thought by appealing to the imagination of the reader.

But neither this, nor any other single test, is sufficient in itself to measure the merit of a work of literature. In order to obtain a valid judgment, a work of literature must be approached from more than one side, and our verdict must be based upon a balance of the results so

[1] The point is fully discussed in chapter iv. p. 71.

obtained. This last test, however, serves one purpose which is worthy of notice. It enables us to discriminate between science and literature. Science is thought embodied in writing ; literature is thought first moulded into form by the idealizing process of the human mind, and then, when so moulded, expressed in writing. Where the idealizing process has been employed by the author, there, in whatever branch of literature it may be, will be the appeal to the imagination of the reader. For this power to affect the imagination reveals the presence of the ' something more ' added by the writer—the presence, that is, of the personal element which raises history or biography to the rank of literature, and lends a new value to the work of the philosopher or the man of science.

II. THE RELATION OF ÆSTHETICS TO CRITICISM

Man discriminates a certain aspect in his surroundings, material and moral, which he designates as ' beautiful ' and refers to the quality of ' beauty.' In conventional language beauty is said to produce sensations and emotions which differ from those produced by the pleasures of sense, while, on the other hand, they do not coincide with the satisfaction produced by the consciousness of right conduct. Though all men are conscious of the influence of beauty in some form or other (for even the Bushman has his rock-paintings), most men, even among societies which have reached a high degree of civilization, are prepared to accept the sensations and emotions so distinguished without troubling themselves to inquire into their origin, or asking what their precise value and significance may be. Philosophy has sought to provide answers to these questions, and German philosophy in particular has been occupied with the task of formulating these answers in a manner consistent with metaphysical systems of thought. Hence has arisen the philosophy of the beautiful, or the 'science of æsthetics,' a special product of the German mind, which has for its object to explain both the origin of the general conception of beauty, and the relationship of that conception to both the states of consciousness, on the one hand, and the material existences, on the other, with which it is respectively identified by human intelligence. But it cannot be said that the body of æsthetic doctrine provided by the researches of Kant, Schelling, Hegel, Schiller, and other metaphysical writers, is wholly satisfactory. Something has been added, no doubt, to the results previously obtained by Greek thought, and old principles have been re-stated in transcendental language ; but both the new and the old truths have been connected with abstract conceptions so cumbrous that the science of æsthetics, as thus formulated, has remained practically ineffective as a contribution to the general knowledge of the world.

More important results have, however, been secured by thinkers who have adopted scientific methods of inquiry. Locke's theory of the Association of Ideas revealed the source and manner of production of whole classes of æsthetic enjoyments. Addison translated the doctrines of Locke and Hobbes into the terms of common experience, and applied the results which he obtained to the examination of creative literature. The further advance which has been made since the days of Locke and Addison has proceeded upon the same lines, and it is now recognised that psychology is the true basis upon which any complete and effective æsthetic theory must be founded. Without attempting to trace the several steps in this advance, it is sufficient for our purposes to take the account given by Mr. Herbert Spencer in his chapter on 'Æsthetic Sentiments.' Here, at length, a scientific principle of explanation is provided, which can be applied to the entire field of æsthetic enjoyment without loss of validity or distinctness.

But before considering this account, it is necessary to indicate with more precision the scope of the term 'æsthetics,' and the character of the subject-matter with which it is concerned. For the words 'æsthetic' and 'æsthetics' have acquired meanings which are quite distinct from the original and primary significance of αἴσθησις (perception). The term has undergone a double process. It has been specialised from 'perception' to the 'perception of *beauty*'; and the '*perception* of beauty' has then been generalised to '*consciousness* of. beauty': consciousness, that is, whether due to sensation, perception, or the simulation of sensations or perceptions, or both, through the imagination. I will endeavour to indicate the significance of these three kinds of æsthetic enjoyments by taking three (roughly) typical instances.

I look out from the window of the room in which I write, and my eye rests upon a stretch of grass still fresh with the recent rains, and raised to a vivid tone by a flood of sunshine. It neither warms nor feeds me to look out on this sun-lit stretch of lawn, but the sensation which the sight of it produces is nevertheless one of enjoyment. Again, from the same window my eye rests upon a line of buildings. The architect's design is such that it satisfies both the desire for unity by the repetition of certain parts, and the desire for variety by the introduction of detail into the repeated parts. Moreover, it is an ancient building, for the whole structure is coloured and harmonised by the hand of time, and, as I look, the pictures of scenes enacted in bygone days arise without conscious effort in my mind. The enjoyment which I now experience is due not merely to sensation, but to both sensation and perception—the perception of qualities which I have learnt by previous experience to recognise as possessing artistic merit and intellectual significance. Once more, I turn from my window to my book-shelves and take down a volume of Shakespeare. I open it at *As You Like It*. As I read I seem to hear the voices of Celia and Rosalind breaking the silence of the forest glades of Arden ; and I grow interested and delighted as I follow the adventures of Rosalind, this girl who is at once so daring and so loving. My enjoyment is no less a fact of consciousness, no less *real* in this sense than it was before ; but it is due neither to a sensation nor a perception, but to the simulation of a series of sensations and perceptions which are suggested to me by the words which I read. This is a species of enjoyment which possesses the characteristic quality of the class of enjoyments termed æsthetic in the highest degree. This quality we will call 'remoteness from physical impulse,' carefully noting, however, that 'impulse' not 'processes' is meant. It is necessary to note this distinction, because æsthetic sensations and perceptions consist largely of physical *processes*, but of physical processes which have been separated from physical *impulses*.

Let me illustrate this quality of 'remoteness from physical impulse' by some examples. The savage sees a roebuck and is glad, because he anticipates the flesh and other useful things with which this beast will supply him when he has killed it. The traveller admires its graceful form, and the splendid activity which it displays as it bounds from rock to rock. Both enjoy the sight of the animal; but the enjoyment of the savage arises from the impulse to kill and eat, that of the traveller is entirely removed from any such primitive desires, and, as being removed from these physical impulses, is disinterested, and therefore æsthetic. But if the traveller seeks to kill the roebuck, either because he has lost his way and is in want of food, or from love of sport, or because he wishes to secure the skin of the animal for purposes of trade, his enjoyment at the sight of the animal ceases to be æsthetic. It becomes at once connected with aims directly arising out of the physical impulses which appear in their primitive form in the savage. Similarly, the pleasure which the millionaire experiences from the sight of his newly-built palace arises from the sense of possession; from the knowledge that this fine house will materially aid him in the realization of his ambition for power and social prestige. The artist and the man of taste also derive pleasure from the sight of the millionaire's house; but their pleasure is solely due to a perception of its artistic merits, and being entirely disconnected from any prospect of material benefit is therefore æsthetic.

But in the sight of a picture, in the sight of a building, in the sound of music, although there is æsthetic pleasure, yet the æsthetic pleasure is directly dependent upon the

senses, since it arises immediately from a sense-percep-
tion, and ceases to be felt when the external stimulus is
removed. The class of æsthetic pleasures with which
literature is concerned do not depend upon any external
stimuli except those which convey the symbols of thought
to eye or ear. The enjoyment, therefore, which comes
from the simulation of sensations or perceptions through
the thoughts of others, or through the co-operation of
the thoughts of others with our own memory and imagination, is the highest, though by no means the most
complete or intense form of æsthetic enjoyment. It is
the most independent of external stimuli, and therefore
the most remote from physical impulse, and the most closely
connected with the mind of the individual. Such pleasures
are in the highest degree free ; they can be enjoyed almost
without reference to external circumstances, and they
are in a peculiar sense the property of the individual
himself : indeed they become part of his personality,
a rich possession of which nothing short of the decay
of his mental powers can deprive him.

As physical impulses are most intimately associated
with the lower forms of human activity, we have here
a principle of discrimination which is supported equally
by the authority of Greek thought and the researches of
modern science.

The disinterested (or disengaged) exercise of the
faculties arising from σχολή (leisure), was emphatically
associated in the Greek mind with the attainment of
a higher standard, both of individual and civic, or
national, development. With Aristotle 'leisure' is an
essential element in happiness,[1] and he ranks the life of

[1] Ethics Nic., 1177ᵇ.

contemplation above the life of practical virtue, chiefly on the ground that leisure, with the associated qualities of self-sufficiency and disinterestedness, penetrates the activities of which that life is made up. And from a more practical point of view he denies the rights of citizenship to the working man, because a life in which the lower activities are exclusively brought into play is a fatal bar to moral and intellectual development.[1]

Mr. Herbert Spencer similarly finds dissociation from elementary and practical needs to be the characteristic quality of æsthetic pleasure. Whereas, however, the Greek view is based mainly upon sociological data, Mr. Herbert Spencer's account has a definite foundation in biology. Æsthetic pleasures, he says,[2] are produced by actions of the faculties of sensation which are ' dissociated from life-serving functions.' His description of æsthetic consciousness is almost identical with the Greek conception of the higher life of contemplation. It arises ' in cases where actions apart from ends form the object-matter.'[3] The origin of æsthetic sensations—and the method in which works of art and other embodiments of the faculties which minister to æsthetic enjoyments affect us—is rendered plain by an adaptation of Schiller's assertion of the connection of æsthetic enjoyments with the universal impulse to ' play.'[4] Æsthetic products, he

[1] Pol., 1278ᵃ.

[2] *Principles of Psychology*, vol. ii., ' Æsthetic Sensations.'

[3] So too Kant: Beauty is a modification of purpose (Zweckmässigkeit) which has no end in view.

[4] Schiller resolves the impulse to play (Spieltrieb) into a union of (1) the impulse to materialise (Stofftrieb), and (2) the impulse to formalise (Formtrieb). The first of these impels us to convert our thought into substance, and the second, to give form or shape to this substance.

says, afford 'substituted activities' for the higher powers of man, just as games and other forms of play do for the lower. Hence the distinction between the 'good' and the 'beautiful.' The consciousness of good arises from genuine activities pursued with a serious purpose in view; that is, when 'actions are realised to be productive of results.' The consciousness of beauty arises from substituted activities pursued merely for their own sake; that is, when 'actions are realised merely without regard to results, but as a source of pleasure.'

That is to say, together with the substituted activities there are substituted pleasures. These pleasures arise be-cause we imagine, through association of ideas, or through less distinct psychological processes, that we are experiencing the actual results of the original activities. But in so far as this state of consciousness has a subjective reality, the imagined pleasures have a validity of their own. This validity, which constitutes æsthetic enjoyment, while it differs on the one hand from the happiness of successful effort, and, on the other, from the satisfaction of desire, approaches in varying degrees of closeness to both the one and the other. But the distinction is never entirely obliterated; it may be detected in the most intense form of æsthetic excitement by the application of the test of remoteness from physical impulse.

The secondary or representative element indicated by this analysis is so conspicuous and important a part of the sum of consciousness which constitutes æsthetic enjoyment, that a clear statement of Mr. Herbert Spencer's account of its character and effects is necessary.

In the first place it is present in the case of simple æsthetic feelings; that is, of sensations as opposed to perceptions. The representative element is in this case permanent or constitutional. It is due partly to inherited (or organic), and partly to acquired (or personal) experience.

'While pleasures and pains,' says Mr. Herbert Spencer, 'are partly constituted of those local and conspicuous elements of feeling directly aroused by special stimuli, they are largely, if not mainly, composed of secondary elements of feeling aroused indirectly by diffused stimulation of the nervous system. From this it is a corollary that a sensorial stimulation such as is produced by a fine colour or a sweet tone, implying as we here infer a large amount of normal action of the parts concerned, without any drawback from excessive action, and thus involving a powerful diffused discharge of which no component is in excess, will tend to arouse a secondary vague pleasure. Æsthetic feelings in general are largely composed of the undefinable consciousness hence arising.' [1]

In æsthetic perceptions—the second order of æsthetic enjoyments—both the primary or presentative, and the secondary or representative element, are present, but they are now no longer simple but complex in character. The presentative element is produced by groups of stimuli, and the representative element contains, besides the effects of diffused stimulation, more precise effects, due to 'a partial revival of various *special* qualifications connected in experience with combinations of the kind presented.' That is to say, the principle of the association of ideas is now actively brought into operation.

It is by virtue of the representative element, therefore, that both a sensation and a perception can become æsthetic.

[1] Ib. p. 636.

But in an æsthetic sensation, and in an æsthetic perception, the presentative element is necessary and forms the basis of the æsthetic enjoyment. There remains a third class of æsthetic feelings in which the relative importance of the two elements is reversed. In æsthetic emotions, which Mr. Herbert Spencer calls the 'highest order' of æsthetic feelings, the representative element is essential and the presentative element incidental; for such forms of æsthetic enjoyment are experienced in states of consciousness which are 'exclusively re-representative' and which are 'reached *through* sensations and perceptions.'

It will be observed that Mr. Herbert Spencer bases his classification of æsthetic pleasures—into sensational, perceptional, and emotional—upon the extent of the representative element. In those chapters in the sequel which deal with Addison's criticism it will be found that I have expressed the opinion [1] that the application of the theory of association of ideas to the study of literature permanently differentiated modern from ancient criticism. For this application led Addison to discover a new test of poetic merit—the appeal to the imagination—and to substitute this for the Greek test of symmetry, upon which Aristotle's doctrine of the supremacy of the plot was based. The significance of this change lies in the fact that the power of appealing to the imagination is a test which touches that element of æsthetic enjoyment to which creative literature can most effectively contribute. It provided, moreover, a measure of poetic merit which could be applied not merely to tragedy or epic, but to every species of creative literature irrespective

[1] P. 52.

of form. In other words, whereas the Greek test of symmetry was a test of artistic merit in general, and was only applicable to creative literature in a secondary degree, the appeal to the imagination was a test not of artistic merit in general, but of that form of artistic merit of which literature was most capable ; and it was, therefore, applicable to literature primarily and specifically.

This opinion was, of course, based solely upon the study of literary methods ; but it is interesting to find that it is supported by the scientific analysis of the psychological processes by which states of æsthetic enjoyment are created. Another opinion to which I have also given expression [1]—that prose-fiction, and not verse, is destined to become the supreme vehicle for the conveyance of poetic thought—is also confirmed in the passage in which Mr. Herbert Spencer indicates the conditions under which literature, in its various forms, produces æsthetic emotion.

This passage, which I quote in full, is in other respects valuable as indicating with singular directness the part which literature plays in æsthetic consciousness, and, therefore, the relationship of criticism to æsthetics. Æsthetics deal with the entire field of æsthetic enjoyment ; but inasmuch as the supreme merit of literature is to produce the highest order of æsthetic feelings, no sound criticism can afford to neglect the evidence afforded by the study of the states of consciousness with which the science of the beautiful is primarily concerned.

'Recognising the simple æsthetic pleasures derivable from rhythm and euphony, which are explicable in ways above indicated [*i.e.* by force of association, 'when the emotion suggested

[1] P. 210.

by a cadence is a joyous one, opportunity is given for pleasurable sympathy,' &c.], the feelings of beauty yielded by poetry are feelings remotely re-representative ; not only in the sense that they are initiated by ideas or representations, but also in the sense that the sentiments indirectly aroused are representative, often in a high degree. And in prose-fiction, where the vehicle used yields no appreciable sensuous gratification, this re-representativeness of the feelings awakened is complete. A condition to æsthetic pleasure in these higher ranges of it, as in the lower, is that there shall be excited great masses and varieties of the elements out of which the emotions are compounded, while none of them shall be excited in undue degrees. A large volume of emotion without painful intensity in any part, is the effect which a successful drama, or poem, or novel, produces. It is true that success is often measured by the intensity of the resulting feeling—especially pitiful feeling ; though even here the effect may be lost if this feeling is over-taxed by too continuous an appeal. But noting such cases, it must still be held that æsthetic pleasure, properly so called, is the highest when the emotional consciousness has not only breadth and mass, but a variety such as leaves behind no satiety or exhaustion.' [1]

The most perfect form of æsthetic excitement is, according to Mr. Herbert Spencer, that which is caused by a union of the three orders—sensational, perceptional, and emotional—of æsthetic gratification.

' Of course, the most perfect form of æsthetic excitement is reached when these three orders of sensational, perceptional, and emotional gratification are given, by the fullest actions of the respective faculties, with the least deduction caused by painful excess of action.' [2]

This decision has an interesting bearing upon the character of the Drama. The view which it embodies is

[1] Ib., p. 642.   [2] Ib., p. 645.

in entire agreement with an opinion of Aristotle, which is expressed in the course of his discussion in the *Poetics* of the relative merits of Tragedy and Epic as forms of poetry. In this passage [1] he decides in favour of Tragedy on the ground that it has all that Epic has, 'and a very considerable addition in music and scenic accessories : and it is music,' he adds, 'which gives the greatest vividness to the combination of pleasurable emotions produced by Tragedy.' It also supports the view which I have taken of the drama as a *composite* art,[2] in the course of which I have put forward the contention that the perfecting of stage-presentation (which is so marked a feature of the modern drama) does not necessarily involve any loss of artistic dignity. This contention is based upon the opinion that the line of progress of the drama lies in the direction of increased actuality, since the perfecting of its simulation of the real, and the corresponding intensity of the æsthetic sensations which it arouses, form its characteristic merit as a branch of art.

The following passage—which immediately succeeds the sentences quoted above—has a significant bearing upon a question which is discussed in the chapter on 'Authority in Literature.' The opinion is there expressed that the ultimate test of merit in literature must be the 'general sense' of mankind, as opposed to the test of artistic excellence which is embodied in the doctrine of 'art for art's sake.' It will be seen that Mr. Herbert Spencer here applies the same test as a means of deciding the final value of works of art.

'Such an æsthetic excitement is rarely experienced, for the reason that works of art rarely possess all the required

---

[1] 1462ª.   [2] See Chapter X.

characters. Very generally a rendering that is artistic in one respect, goes along with a rendering that is in other respects inartistic. And where the *technique* is satisfactory, it does not commonly happen that the emotion appealed to is of a high order. Measuring æsthetic sentiments and the correlative works of art by the above standards, we find ourselves compelled to relegate to a comparatively inferior place, much that now stands highest. Beginning with the epic of the Greeks and their representations in sculpture of kindred stories, which appeal to feelings of egoistic and ego-altruistic kinds ; passing through middle-age literature, similarly pervaded by inferior sentiments, and through the pictures of the old masters, which by the ideas and feelings they excite very rarely compensate for the disagreeable shocks they give to perceptions cultivated by the study of appearances ; down to many admired works of modern art, which, good in *technique*, are low in the emotions they express and arouse, such as the battle scenes of Vernet and the pieces of Gerôme, which alternate between the sensual and the sanguinary—we see that in one or other of the required attributes, they nearly all fall short of the forms of art corresponding to the highest forms of æsthetic feeling.' [1]

It remains to notice one further point which is suggested by Mr. Herbert Spencer's account of the origin of æsthetic sentiments. The demand for the limitation of the hours of labour, and for the provision of extended opportunities for mental culture, which together form one of the foremost of the ideals of modern democracy, receives a new significance when we recognise the biological basis for the connection between art and leisure. For scientific analysis makes it plain that æsthetic enjoyment, whether in the individual or in the

[1] Ib., pp. 645–6.

community, is only possible when there is ' an organization so superior that the energies have not to be wholly expended in the fulfilment of material requirements from hour to hour.'[1] Æsthetic activity, therefore, depends directly upon the economic management of the physical and mental faculties : and since political, social, and biological development alike tend to produce this result, it is clear that, with the progress of humanity, art and literature will occupy an increasingly important place in the life of man. Democracy, therefore, instead of destroying, must tend to foster art.

[1] Ib., p. 647.

CHAPTER I

PLATO CONSIDERS LITERATURE AS A VEHICLE OF KNOWLEDGE

If we cast about for a convenient starting-point from which to approach an inquiry into the nature and methods of literature, we could scarcely do better than select the famous saying of Descartes, *Cogito ergo sum*. But whereas originally man derived the sensations which constitute his being exclusively from the direct action of material existences, he now derives them in part from the previous sensations of other men preserved and embodied in custom, literature and art. From this point of view—that is to say, if we regard man primarily as a sentient being— literature is an element in human life which is of ever-increasing importance.

But literature had existed for a long time, and had attained a high state of development, before it won any permanent recognition as chief among our secondary sources of sensation. The first conscious acknowledgment in literature of its own existence, as a serious contributor to the sum total of human life, marks the commencement of criticism ; and this acknowledgment naturally grew out of the reflective philosophy of Plato. In the search for truth, which he conducted through the powerful instrument of dialectic, Plato found that men derive their opinions and their rules of conduct from a knowledge of literature as well as from a knowledge of life. He recognised especially that literature is the medium by which the young are introduced to the world, and inferior minds are enabled to share the wisdom of their superiors; and he was, therefore, compelled, in constructing a system of morals, to take account both of the subject-matter and of the forms of this source of knowledge.

It is not surprising that a criticism conceived on such a basis should be inadequate.

What Jowett has written of his work in general is true of his work in the special field of criticism. 'He is no dreamer, but a great philosophical genius struggling with the unequal conditions of light and knowledge under which he is living.'[1] And so in Plato we find a remarkable, almost instinctive, comprehension of the true principles which underlie the development of art and literature, joined to a fatal misconception of the character and limitations of artistic representation, and, we must add, of the work of the Greek poets.

The contrast between Plato and Aristotle in their respective researches in the department of criticism is very significant. Plato is an idealist, and his criticism is an examination of literature and art in the light of principles deduced from the study of the life of man. Aristotle is a realist, and his criticism is based upon a consideration of the actual literary material which lay before him. Plato appears to have regarded the productions of art and literature for critical purposes solely as a vehicle for conveying philosophic truth; and criticism meant for him an endeavour to ascertain how far the

---

[1] *Dialogues*, Pref. p. ix.

message of poetry and the arts agreed with the message of philosophy. The desire to reach the truth directed and controlled the whole of his vast intellectual activity, and when he applies himself to art and literature this motive is so predominant that it obscures his appreciation of the lesser elements of beauty and pleasure, and prevents him from realising the difference between truth in art and truth in nature. Art was a vehicle by which men could be taught the truths of philosophy, and the only object of criticism, as he conceived it, was to find out to what extent it fulfilled this purpose.

Aristotle's criticism, on the other hand, was independent of any ethical motive; under his scheme it formed a separate and distinct department of inquiry. An art, he says in the *Ethics*,[1] is the product of 'a union of a creative faculty and reason.' In the *Poetics* he finds that the source of the creative faculty is the primitive impulse of imitation ; and he points out that art as thus analysed must produce results which can be distinguished from the results of any mere effort of the understanding.

As a contribution to a specific department of human knowledge, Aristotle's account of the origin and methods of art in the *Poetics* shows an infinite advance upon Plato's exposure of its defects in the *Republic*. But Plato's method, being in fact the method of art itself, by employing the powerful assistance of the imagination, enabled him to pierce more deeply into the heart of things, and to reveal truths of higher import and wider application than the truths disclosed by the more exact but more restricted investigations of Aristotle. And so it has come about that while the rules of Aristotle, based upon a limited

[1] 1140a.

area of observation, have been gradually superseded, the principles of Plato are seen to be in harmony with the modern conception of the functions of art and literature. For the time has come when art and literature are no longer the property of the few, but when in fact they are as intimately a part of the life of civilized peoples, as they were of Hellenic life in the age of Pericles ; and, therefore, the identity of their spirit with the spirit of the truest thought and the highest conduct—which Plato asserted to be the true relation between them and the life of man—seems no longer impossible of realisation, but has, on the contrary, come to be regarded as the natural goal of their development.

Of Plato's general criticism it is sufficient to note that the opinions scattered throughout the *Dialogues* anticipate the artistic principles laid down by Aristotle in the *Poetics* in more than one important particular. For example, the doctrine that both the incidents and the characters represented by the poet should be typical, appears more than once in the *Poetics* in the form of a statement that, according to the method of poetry, 'an impossibility which is credible is preferable to a possibility which is incredible.'[1] Now in the *Phaedrus*, Plato not only formulates the same principle with respect to the special art, Rhetoric, which he is there discussing, but he carries the argument a step further, by showing how this principle can be reconciled to what he calls the 'first quality' or 'condition precedent' of good speaking—namely, 'that the mind of the speaker should know the truth of what he is about to speak.'[2] This he does by pointing out that the man who knows the truth of what he

[1] 1461b.   [2] P. 259 (St.).

describes, knows best how to produce those resemblances which prove so persuasive. For, 'if a man does not know what the facts are in each case, he cannot possibly acquire the master's manner of gradually leading his audience from the fact to the opposite of the fact by means of resemblances or analogous instances ; nor can he see through the speech of a rival who employs the same method.' [1]

Again, Aristotle repeatedly insists upon the supreme importance of the plot as an element of Tragedy. Plato insists upon the same doctrine in his discussion of Rhetoric ; and in so doing he uses the same figure— that of an organism—which Aristotle uses to enforce his meaning in the *Poetics*. 'Every speech,' Plato says, 'ought to be composed like a living thing, having its own body and being deficient neither in head nor feet ; both the trunk and the extremities of the speech must be so composed as to harmonise with one another and with the whole.' [2] And he adds two qualities which distinguish all correct literary construction : 'First, to group the scattered facts, drawn from many sources, in a single idea, by regarding them from one point of view . . . ; and then to be able to treat them again singly under natural divisions—hitting the joints in fact instead of breaking off portions like a bad carver.' [3] And he subsequently extends the principle from a speech to a tragedy ; for the art of tragedy does not consist in the composition of a number of separate speeches, but in 'the arranging of these elements in a harmonious and consistent whole.'

But these are, after all, points of minor importance.

[1] 262.   [2] 264.   [3] 265.

What is essential for us to know in Plato's criticism is, first, the nature of those deeper and more pregnant principles revealed by his idealistic method ; and, secondly, the manner in which he applies these principles to Greek art and poetry. The former contains what is most permanent and most remarkable in his inquiries ; in the latter, the extent of his misapprehension of the method of artistic representation—and the consequent value of Aristotle's contribution to the science of criticism—appears most clearly.

The permanent element in Plato's criticism is contained in three mutually dependent principles. In literature the 'thought' is prior to the 'form' ; greatness in art depends upon morality in the artist ; and art and morals are mutually connected, both in the sense that the character of the artist appears in the character of his work, and in the sense that the creations of art have an influence upon the life of man which can be expressed in terms of morality.

The first of these principles is most clearly stated in the message of the *Phaedrus*, which is addressed to literature as a whole.

'Go you to Lysias and say that we two have gone down to the fountain of the Nymphs and the seat of the Muses, and have held speech with them ; and that they bade us tell him and other composers of speeches, and Homer and other composers of poetry, whether set to music or not, and Solon, too, and others who have committed political compositions to writing under the name of laws, that if, in composing these various works, they knew where the truth was, and could make good their statements in case of their being called in question, and, if they maintain that they are able to prove by word of mouth much more than their writings contain—if this be so, we must tell them they have no business to be called by any of the names appropriated to these several classes of composers—orator, poet, or legislator—but that they should be called by a name which expresses the purpose on which they have really been engaged : and this purpose is the search for " wisdom," and their name is " lover of wisdom," or philosopher.' [1]

The principle of the interdependence of art and morals is asserted in its widest form in the third book of the *Republic*. Here he lays down the general standard by which the fitness of poetry and the arts for admission into the ideal commonwealth is to be tested ; and he decides that a thing is beautiful just so far as it is made to be an expression of morality.

' Then excellence of thought, and of harmony, and of form, and of rhythm, is connected with excellence of character, with good nature, that is, not in the sense of the colourless character which we euphemistically term " good nature," but in that of the disposition which is really well and nobly equipped from the point of view of character. . . .
'The qualities which are implied in this excellence of character are conspicuously present in painting and all similar arts, in weaving and embroidery and architecture, and, indeed, in the productions of all the lesser arts, and further in the constitution of bodies and of all organic growths. In all of these excellence or defectiveness of form can be discerned. And defectiveness of form and rhythm and harmony are associated with deficiencies of thought and of character, while the corresponding artistic excellences are associated with the

[1] 278. [The form of the passage has been slightly altered in translation.]

corresponding moral excellences of self-restraint and goodness ; indeed, they are directly expressive of them.

' If this be so, we must not confine our supervision to our poets. In addition to compelling the poets to embody the stamp of morality in their productions as a condition of their working among us, we must exercise supervision over the whole class of art-workers. We must prevent them from embodying this expression of vice or moral obliquity or meanness or bad-taste either in their representations of living things or in their buildings, or in anything else which they produce. If we cannot restrain them, we must not allow them to produce among us at all, for we are bound to prevent our " guardians " from being bred upon the images of vice, like cattle on rank grass, gathering many impressions from many sources, day by day and little by little, and feeding upon them, and so unconsciously collecting a great mass of evil in their souls. Instead of this we must look for artists who are able out of the goodness of their own natures to trace the nature of beauty and perfection, that so our young men, like persons who live in a healthy place, may be perpetually influenced for good. Every impression which they receive through eye or ear will come from embodiments of beauty, and this atmosphere, like the health-giving breeze which flows from bracing regions, will imperceptibly lead them from their earliest childhood into association and harmony with the spirit of Truth, and into love for that spirit.' [1]

Such a censorship is, of course, fatal to artistic freedom in general, while in respect of poetry it excludes ' the indiscriminate realist ' ; the man ' whose cleverness makes him capable of assuming every form and reproducing every object.' To such a dramatic artist the citizens of the ideal commonwealth are merciless. His

[1] *Republic*, pp. 400–1 (St.).

talent is freely admitted, but he is told that 'one like him neither does, nor indeed *can*, exist' there. Elsewhere he may be welcome, but for their part they have profit not pleasure in view, and they will therefore require a 'more austere and less delightful poet,' who will take virtue for his model and cast his poetry into an educational mould.[1]

Plato has already shown the need for this censorship by a consideration of the subject-matter of Homer and other poets.[2] In the case of Homer, he selects a number of passages which attribute various kinds of immoral conduct to the gods and heroes. He takes instances in which the characters display terror at death, sexual irregularities, cowardice, deceitfulness, insubordination, covetousness, and unmanly or immoderate emotion. Such passages he condemns, first, as 'sacrilegious and untrue,' and, secondly, 'morally hurtful to the hearers.' In addition to this, he brings against literature a general charge of immorality. 'Poets and prose-writers,' he says, 'are mistaken in dealing with human life in the most important respects. They give us to understand that many evil livers are happy and many righteous men unhappy; and that wrong-doing, if it be undetected, is profitable, while honest dealing is beneficial to one's neighbour, but damaging to one's self.'[3]

Thus far Plato confines himself, in the main, to a criticism of the subject-matter of poetry. All art must be an expression of morality, but poetry, he finds, so far from expressing morality, has become a vehicle for conveying immoral notions. In the tenth book of the *Republic* he formulates his charges more definitely. He

[1] 398.   [2] 386–391.   [3] 392.

not only complains of the subject-matter of the poets, but condemns the form and method of the poetic representation of the facts of life.

In this fuller criticism he charges poetry with two inherent defects—unreality, and a tendency to foster the emotional element in man to the detriment of the rational.

But before considering this fuller criticism it is necessary to know how far Plato agrees with Aristotle in accepting imitation ($\mu\iota\mu\eta\sigma\iota\varsigma$) as the basis of poetry. For this purpose we may refer to a passage in the third book of the *Republic*, where he roughly classifies different kinds of poetic composition by reference to the use of imitation.

' In poetry,' he says, ' whether the plot be invented or consist of traditional stories, there is one style of representation which consists solely of " imitation "—to take your examples, tragedy and comedy—and another which consists of the narrative of the poet himself—dithyrambic poetry is perhaps the best example ; while epic poetry is one of many instances of a third style which employs both dialogue and narrative.' [1]

It appears, therefore, that whereas Aristotle finds in ' imitation ' the basis of all creative literature, whether dramatic or not in form, Plato calls ' imitative ' only so much of a literary composition as is written in character. In other words, the difference between the meaning respectively attached to the term by Plato and Aristotle is, broadly, the difference between ' imitative ' and ' reproductive.'

Now, in advancing his first charge—that of unreality

[1] 394.

—against poetry, Plato is influenced by the restricted and more elementary meaning which he attaches to μίμησις. He endeavours to establish the existence of this first defect at the outset by an analysis of the nature of knowledge in harmony with his own philosophic theory of 'ideas.' Taking the commonplace example of a bed, he proceeds to distinguish three forms—the 'idea' or archetype, the actual piece of furniture so-called, and the artistic reproduction, owing their existence respectively to God, to the upholsterer, and to the artist.[1] Like this last the poet is neither creator nor artificer, but merely an imitator of the latter's work, and, being such, his work is two degrees removed from the original creation of God. But Plato is not content with this theoretic proof; he proposes a practical test. If the poet really knows the truth of what he describes, and does not merelyr repoduce other people's knowledge, he must have given some actual demonstration of his possession of such knowledge. And so he asks the question of Homer :

'Homer, if you are not twice removed from truth in respect of virtue (as being the producer of a representation and, therefore, an imitator as we have defined the term), but once only, and if you were therefore capable of knowing what practices make men respectively better or worse as individuals and as members of a state, can you tell us of any city which has received an improved constitution from you, in the sense in which Lacedaemon was improved by Lycurgus, and many other cities, both great and small, were improved by many other men ? What city acknowledges its indebtedness to you as a righteous lawgiver and a general benefactor ? Italy and

[1] 597.

Sicily thus acknowledge Charondas, and we Solon; does any
community acknowledge you?'[1]

Naturally Homer is compelled to admit that he has
done nothing of the kind; and he subsequently gives
most satisfactory evidence towards establishing the point,
that 'all poets from Homer downwards imitate phantoms
of virtue and whatever else they select as their subjects,
without ever coming into contact with the truth.'

But not only are the creations of poetry unreal, and
therefore useless for practical purposes; they appeal to
the unreasoning and emotional part of man's nature.

In framing this second charge Plato first states with
singular clearness the objects which poetry, or creative
literature, especially strives to reproduce. They are
'men engaged in actions either involuntary or voluntary,
attributing their good or bad fortune to these actions, and
in all of them displaying either grief or joy.'[2] But the
poets, he continues, in representing human action give
exhibitions not of good, but of bad conduct. They are
compelled to do so by the requirements of their artistic
method. In the first place, 'the irascible temperament
admits of constant and varied reproduction, while the
wise and quiet temperament, which scarcely ever varies,
is neither easily reproduced nor, when reproduced, readily
comprehended.'[3] And in the next, the poet like the
painter 'associates with an element of the soul which is
as depraved as he, and not with its noblest element.'[4]
It is the evil result of this constant exhibition of depravity
which forms the culminating count of the indictment—
'for, that poetry should be capable of injuring even good

[1] 599.　　　[2] 603.　　　[3] 604.　　　[4] 605.

men, with the exception of a very small minority, is a matter of terrible importance.'[1]

The manner in which this injurious effect is brought about is described in relation to that feeling of 'fear and pity,' which is produced by witnessing a representation of the disasters of the imagined persons ; and the production of which is regarded by Aristotle as the special function of tragedy, or poetry in its highest form.

'The part of the soul which is forcibly kept down in the case of our own misfortunes, and which craves to weep and bewail itself without stint and take its fill of grief, being so constituted as to find satisfaction in these emotions, is the very part which is filled and pleased by the poets ; while that which is naturally the noblest part of us, because it is not adequately disciplined by reason and habit, relaxes its guard over this emotional part, representing to itself that the sufferings which it contemplates are not part of itself, and that there is no shame in its praising and pitying the unseasonable grief of another who professes to be a good man. On the contrary, the pleasure which it experiences it considers to be so much gain, and it will not allow its contempt for the poem as a whole to rob it of this pleasure. For only a very few can realise that the character of our own emotions must be affected by the manner in which we participate in the emotions of others. Yet it is so, for if we let our own sense of pity grow strong by feeding upon the griefs of others, it is not easy to restrain it in the case of our own sufferings.'[2]

And what applies to pity applies also to love and anger, and to all the manifestations of desire, pain, and pleasure ; for poetic imitation 'waters and cherishes the passions when they ought to wither, and makes them govern

[1] 605.   [2] 606.

when they ought to be kept in subjection, in order that we may become better and happier, instead of worse and more miserable.'[1]

There are two considerations, however, which explain in part, though they do not justify, the severity of Plato's criticism of Greek poetry and the Greek poets.

In the first place, it is necessary to remember the importance of the function which Greek poetry in general, and the Greek drama in particular, was called upon to perform. At the time at which Plato wrote, and in the society to which he addressed himself, the poetry of Homer and Hesiod, and the representations of the dramatists, performed functions which are to-day entrusted to agencies as diverse as the pulpit, the press, the stage, and literature in general. And if Plato, in asking from poetry the high morality of the professor of religion, the practical knowledge of the 'fourth estate,' and the enchantments of fancy, was asking too much, the fault lay as much in circumstances as in himself. In the second place, he had a great love of poetry. Like an ardent lover he not only sees keenly, but feels bitterly, the defects in his mistress. And in making his estimate of the qualities of poetry this bitterness is uppermost in his mind, and makes his criticism proportionately severe. But even thus, when he hardens his heart and deals roughly with her, the underlying tenderness will at times appear. He will be glad if a reconciliation can be effected. He is eager for some literary champion to appear, and prove him in the wrong; 'for the cause of righteousness will gain much, if poetry can be made the vehicle of duty as well as of pleasure.'[2]

[1] 606.　　　　[2] 607.

What is really the most serious fault in this estimate of poetry, considered as a piece of literary criticism, is the failure to recognise and appreciate what was good in the poets whose works were before him : the fact that only the bad is selected, the immoral actions of the gods, and the deceitfulness, cowardice, and unscrupulous action of the heroes in Homer, and the exaggeration and mis-representation of the appeal to the emotions in the drama. It was, perhaps, only natural that he should express no admiration for a beauty of style, and a structural per-fection, which were elementary characteristics of Greek art, but how can we pardon him for giving no hint of the interpretative power of Æschylus' $\dot{a}\nu\dot{\eta}\rho\iota\theta\mu o\nu$ $\gamma\dot{\epsilon}$-$\lambda a\sigma\mu a$; or of the lyric sweetness of Sophocles' 'Love unconquered . . . '; or of the supreme pathos of the death of the faithful hound that raised himself in recog-nition of his master, Odysseus, and then lay down to die ? Why does he tell us nothing of the splendid presentation of the doctrine of retribution for sin given by the Attic tragedians, or of the portraiture of Nausicaa's innocence, and Penelope's constancy, by Homer ? Was there no moral purpose to be discerned here ? Nevertheless the ideal of a literature which, in point of teaching, is indis-tinguishable from philosophy, embodies a loftier con-ception of the functions of poetry than any which is contained in the *Poetics*, and it is one which, as I have already remarked, is essentially in harmony with our modern aspirations.

How was it, then, that Plato, having got so far, failed in his criticism of Greek poetry to discern the con-nection between the 'imaginative reason' and the spiritual teachings of philosophy ? Probably because the

common conception of human life prevalent in the
Hellenic era was one in which man's activity was regarded as coterminous with his physical existence, and
it was only a reflection of this kind of life that was expected in poetry.   It was just here that his misconception of the character of artistic representation, as shown
in the charge of unreality which he brings against poetry
and art, was most disastrous.   He assumed that poetry
and art, being only imitations of material existences,
could contain nothing but a reflection of this common
conception of the life of man.   To adopt the form of a
remark of Aristotle, he first assumed that the poets' view
of life was material, and then blamed them because their
view, being spiritual, did not answer the tests of resemblance to material reality by which alone he measured
their work.   In short, Plato, in recognising literature
and art as vehicles of knowledge, assumed that their
method was identical with the method of his own
dialectic : it remained for Aristotle to distinguish between
the method of art and the method of logic, and, in so
doing, to point out in what respect a resemblance between
the productions of art and the external reality upon which
they were based was to be expected.

CHAPTER II

ARISTOTLE CONSIDERS POETRY AS A BRANCH OF ART

ARISTOTLE takes the subject out of the regions of morals and politics, and confines its scope by limitations which arise naturally in the course of his account of the origin and methods of art. His broadest conception of art is, however, to be found in the *Ethics*,[1] where he defines an art as 'a union of a productive faculty and reason.' In the *Poetics* he explains the nature of this dual origin. The 'imitation' which he, in common with Plato, finds to be the basis of its manifestations, is traced to a primitive impulse which can be separated from the love of knowledge ; and he clearly distinguishes between the method of poetry and the method of history, even when they both employ the same instrument—words without metre or musical accompaniment. 'The business of the poet,' he says, ' is to tell not what has happened, but what could happen, and what is possible, either from its probability, or from its necessary connection with what has gone before. The historian and the poet do not differ in using or not using metre—for the writings of Herodotus could be put into metre without being any the less a history, whether in metre or not—but the difference lies in this fact, that the one tells what has happened and the other what could happen. And, therefore, poetry

---

[1] 1140ᵃ. Ταὐτὸν ἂν εἴη τέχνη καὶ ἕξις μετὰ λόγου ἀληθοῦς ποιητική.

has a wider truth and a higher aim than history ; for poetry deals rather with the universal, history with the particular.' [1] And in distinguishing between the effects of the incidents and of the dialogue in tragedy, he remarks that 'the effects produced by the incidents should be plain without argument, those produced by speech should be the work of the speaker and arise out of his speech.' These latter effects, therefore, belong more properly to the art of rhetoric.[2]

Moreover, there are two passages in which it is possible to discern a direct reply to the first of the charges—that of 'unreality '—which Plato brought against poetry. In speaking of the complaints of critics he says : 'Since the poet is an imitator just as much as a painter or any other image-maker, he must in all cases reproduce things in one of three aspects—as they w re or are, as men say they are and they seem to be, or as they ought to be.' And he adds : 'It should also be remembered that the standard of correctness differs in politics and poetry as much as it does in any other art and poetry.' [3] The other passage contains the statement that, 'according to the method of poetry, an impossibility which is credible is preferable to a possibility which is incredible.' And this is supported by an illustration from the sister art of painting. The characters of Zeuxis were impossible, but their impossibility made them the more correct, 'for the type should be more perfect than the individual.' [4]

He also finds a reply to the second charge—that poetry pleased and fostered the irrational and emotional part of man's nature to the detriment of the nobler intellectual element—in a dry illustration from the science

[1] 1451b.   [2] 1456b.   [3] 1460b.   [4] 1461b.

of medicine which he attached to his definition of tragedy. 'Tragedy . . . is an imitation of a serious and complete action which has magnitude. The imitation is effected by embellished language, each kind of embellishment varying in the constituent parts. It is acted, not narrated ; and it uses the agency of pity and fear to effect a purging of these and the like emotions.' [1] That is to say, just as humours are carried out of the physical system by medical treatment, so the moral system of the spectator is relieved of an excess of emotion, when emotion is artificially excited in the performance of the tragedy. To work upon the emotional element in man was, therefore, part of the proper function of the art of poetry, and the effect of this appeal to the emotions was equally beneficial and not hurtful.

But these replies to Plato occur incidentally, and in the form of comments upon certain aspects of poetry which arise in the course of his general argument.

In addressing himself to the consideration of poetry as a branch of art, Aristotle first lays down certain elementary characteristics of the process of imitation which are common to art and, therefore, appear in all forms of poetry, or creative literature. Having thus cleared the ground, he proceeds to examine the structure and methods of the one form of poetry, tragedy, which might, or might not, represent the ultimate development of the art, but which, at any rate, contained all the elements found in any known form of poetic composition. These elements are six in number. There is the plot, or contexture of incidents ; the character, or that by which we distinguish the natures of the persons ; the diction in

[1] 1449^b.

which their thoughts are expressed ; the sentiment which animates them ; the stage-representation ; and the music by which the songs of the chorus are accompanied. Of these, the plot, which is repeatedly asserted to be the most important, being successively termed the 'final aim,' the 'soul' and the 'central principle' of tragedy, bears the same relation to the completed poem as the design of a painter bears to his picture.

From this view of tragedy it follows that an ability on the part of the composer to choose a suitable subject is an elementary necessity. That is to say, the poet must know how to select so much human action, and human action of such a character, as admits of being effectively reproduced by the methods of art, and within the limits of the poetic composition in question. Aristotle, therefore, proceeds to state the rules for the composition of this all-important element. But in thus formulating rules for the construction of the plot with reference to the one form, tragedy, which he regards as the highest development of the art of poetry, he is careful to point out where they fail in their application to epic poetry.

The first requirement of the plot is unity. 'As in the other imitative arts the one imitation must have one subject, so, too, the plot, since it is an imitation of an action, must be an imitation of an action that is one and whole, and its separate incidents must be so connected that if one is changed or removed the whole plot is altered and disturbed : for a part which can be added or withdrawn without producing any effect is not a member of the whole.'[1] It must also contain a powerful appeal to the emotions of pity and fear. In order to effect this,

[1] 1451ᵃ.

there must be a change from good to bad fortune, and this change, or disaster, must be so managed as to enlist the sympathies of the spectator in the highest degree.

'The change exhibited must neither be that of good men from good fortune to bad (for this does not arouse fear or pity but disgust), nor that of bad men from bad fortune to good (for this is furthest of all removed from the tragic ideal, for it has nothing that it ought to have; it neither commands sympathy, nor pity, nor fear). Nor, again, should the change be that of an utterly worthless man suddenly hurled from good fortune to bad; for a change so managed would command our sympathy without causing pity or fear. For of these two last emotions, the former is felt in respect of undeserved misfortune, the latter in cases which resemble our own—pity because the suffering is undeserved; fear because the persons who suffer resemble ourselves. And so the situation commands neither pity nor fear. An intermediate character remains. Such a character is one who, without possessing conspicuous virtue or goodness, is overtaken by misfortune, not through vice or worthlessness, but through some defect, when he is at the height of his reputation and prosperity, as was the case with Œdipus and Thyestes and other notable members of the heroic families.' [1]

Aristotle further distinguishes the kinds of plots, as 'simple' and 'complicated'; 'single' and 'double'; he characterises and discusses 'revolution,' 'recognition,' 'development,' and 'solution'; gives rules for the length of the episodes and for their treatment in relation to the central action, and finally concludes with practical hints for the actual work of composing. It is unnecessary, however, for us to follow him further in this detailed examination, for a mere enumeration of these heads is

[1] 1452ᵇ.

sufficient to indicate the character of the criticism which it contains.

To pass on to the remaining elements into which tragedy is analysed. The second element, character, appears to include any outward manifestation of the will. 'There will be character,' he says, 'if the dialogue or the action reveals some principle of choice, of whatever kind ; and good character if this principle be good.'[1] He then states, with illustrations, the four requisites of character : it must be good, that is, relatively good, appropriate, typical, and consistent. When Aristotle comes to discuss the next two elements, sentiment and diction, he feels that he is travelling beyond the scope of his subject.

'The principles involved in sentiment,' he says, 'have been laid down in my treatise on rhetoric, for the subject is one which belongs more properly to that inquiry. It is concerned with all effects which ought to be produced by speech. These effects may be distinguished as proof, refutation, the production of the emotions of pity, fear, anger, and all such like ; to which must be added the art of heightening or extenuating the bare facts.'[2]

Similarly, in treating of diction, he refers one branch of the subject to 'the actor's art' ; and he then enters upon a discussion which is mainly grammatical. But he includes in this an analysis of 'metaphor' and 'analogy,' and defines the limits within which the use of uncommon words, together with other forms of poetic licence, is permissible. As the enrichment of language is one of the means by which poetry produces its special charm, all this is appropriate enough. It is also worthy of notice that he rightly insists upon the value of metaphor. He

[1] 1454ᵃ.   [2] 1456ᵃ.

pronounces it to be the greatest of these technical aids, and adds that ' it is a proof of natural ability ; for to write good metaphors is to have an eye for analogies.'[1]

Of stage representation he says little ; but what he says is singularly to the point. It is enchanting, ' but it has the least artistic merit and is least closely connected with the art of poetry.'[2] And again, he remarks that ' it is possible to produce fear and pity by sights presented on the stage,' but that the higher method is to produce such effects by ' the actual arrangement of the incidents ' ; for ' to do this by means of the spectacle is inartistic and requires costly appliances.'[3] Music, the remaining element, is ' the greatest of the embellishments.' It is not directly discussed, but in his account of the chorus he condemns the practice of introducing songs which are unconnected with the action of the tragedy.[4]

As tragedy contains all the elements of poetry, the account of Epic is naturally brief. It resolves itself into a statement of the modifications which must be made in applying the rules already given for the construction of the plot, and an examination of the respective merits of the two chief forms of poetry. Aristotle decides that the plot of an epic poem should in general be marked by the same characteristics as the plot of a tragedy, but it has less unity, in proportion as an epic has greater length than a tragedy. Moreover, the instrument of imitation is different ; tragedy is ' imitation by action,' Epic is ' narrative poetry, or imitation by verse.' The effect of this difference is seen in two ways. In the first place, the length of the episodes, and the importance of the sub-

---

[1] . . . Τὸ τὸ ὅμοιον θεωρεῖν ἐστίν. 1459[a].
[2] 1450[b].   [3] 1453[b].   [4] 1456[a].

sidiary action, is increased ; and in the second, the element of the marvellous can be more freely introduced. On the first point Aristotle remarks that, ' in epic poetry the fact that the imitation is effected by narrative makes it possible to represent the simultaneous progress of several divisions of the story, and by these divisions, provided they are relevant, the grandeur of the poem is increased. This is a quality which gives Epic a greater breadth of effect than Tragedy, for it provides variety by introducing contrast into the episodes.'[1] The second point is one which affects the selection of materials. In this respect the epic poet has greater scope than the tragic :

'Tragedies should have an element of marvel, but in Epic there is more room for that improbability which forms so large an element in the marvellous, because the action is not before our eyes. The pursuit of Hector would appear absurd upon the stage—a crowd of Greek soldiers standing without attempting to pursue, and Achilles shaking his head—but in the poem the absurdity is not noticed.'[2]

On the question of the relative merits of Epic and Tragedy as forms of poetry, he decides in favour of the latter :

'for it has all that Epic has—it can use the metre of Epic —and a very considerable addition in music and scenic accessories ; and it is music which gives the greatest vividness to the combination of pleasurable emotions produced by Tragedy.'[3]

The above sentence, which characteristically expresses the Greek view of poetry as a composite art, will suitably conclude this brief outline of the argument of the *Poetics* ;

[1] 1459b.   [2] 1460a.   [3] 1462a.

and we may pause for a moment to consider what Aristotle has done.

By the *Poetics*, Aristotle placed art upon the dual foundation, sense and reason. He distinguished the method of creative literature—whether with or without metre—from the method of history and other branches of literature, which are mere transcripts of reality ; and so separated the truth of art from the truth of logic. He showed that the appeal to the emotions, which Plato blamed, is an essential element in the dominant form of poetry, and proved by a medical analogy and by philosophic analysis that the effect of this appeal was not hurtful but beneficial to the moral nature of man. And lastly, he sketched with masterly precision the outlines of the structure which forms, in a greater or less degree, the external manifestation of every species of poetic composition.

And yet, if we review this criticism—and to enable the reader to do this has been the object of the preceding account of the *Poetics*—we can scarcely fail to see that the conception of poetry which is here presented is less in harmony with the modern conception of poetry than Plato's ideal of an actual identity between it and philosophy. For, by thus considering poetry in close relationship to a form which was capable in the highest degree of external realisation by the senses, Aristotle has gradually invested all forms of poetry with the objective reality of the drama ; and the central test by which it is proposed to measure the merit of poetry is one which is primarily applicable to the work of the painter and the sculptor—symmetry or structural perfection. As we survey the wide field of creative literature which now lies before our mental vision, with all its variety of growth and development, we ask ourselves in dismay, 'How can these rules guide us to that which is the object of criticism—the comprehension of what is best and most permanent in the works of great writers?' For how could Aristotle's tragic measure contain the fulness of the poetic harvest which includes (to omit all lesser names) the works of Virgil, Dante, Milton, and Shakespeare? If he had been charged with neglecting this aspect of criticism, he would have found a ready answer: 'It belongs to another inquiry—ethics, politics, or religion, as the case may be."

Here we touch the line which divides modern criticism from Greek criticism as formulated by Aristotle. When we criticise we ask first, 'What is the thought?' When the Greeks criticised, they asked first, 'What is the form?' In other words, we have adopted the standpoint of poetry itself; and so long as we find in it 'the finer spirit of all knowledge,' we are content to believe that Nature herself will provide an appropriate vehicle for its utterances.

CHAPTER III

INCOMPLETE and partial, however, as was this formal criticism of Aristotle, it was nevertheless the last word of the ancient world. In all departments of intellectual activity, with the sole exception of the science of law, Rome was the child of Greece; and no addition was made to this last word of Hellenism until the intellect of Europe had first been stirred to productiveness by the Renaissance, and this period of productiveness had in turn been succeeded by a period of reflection. Then, when men began to take stock of the new literature, which had been added to the recovered literature of Greece and Rome, it was upon the foundation of Aristotle's treatise that criticism was reconstructed. During the seventeenth and the earlier part of the eighteenth century, its canons were accepted as supreme. At this time France was the leader of European thought, and Greece was the schoolmistress of France. 'Following, or thinking they followed the ancients,' says Mr. Saintsbury,[1] 'French dramatists and dramatic critics adopted certain fixed rules according to which a poet had to write just as a whist-player has to play the game.'[2]

[1] *History of French Literature*, p. 303.
[2] Even in Addison we read[1] ' . . . although in Poetry it be abso-

---

[1] *Spectator*, No. 409.

Meanwhile in England, where the literary harvest of the Renaissance had been most ample, one mind had penetrated the secret of poetic success, and one voice had stated with perfect clearness the philosophic basis which gives superior truth and value to the poetic treatment of the facts of life.

'Poesy . . . is nothing else but Feigned History, which may be styled as well in prose as in verse. The use of this

lutely necessary that the unities of time, place, and action, with other points of the same nature, should be thoroughly explained and understood.' Now, as a matter of fact, of these three dramatic unities—time, place, and action—Aristotle gives an elastic rule for the first, omits to mention the second, and speaks fully only of the third. The elastic rule is contained in the cautiously expressed *obiter dictum* which occurs in a comparison of the period of action in Epic and Tragedy. 'Further,' he says,[1] 'in the period of the action, while Tragedy endeavours to confine itself to a single revolution of the sun, or to only slightly exceed that limit, Epic is unlimited in point of time.' In speaking of the third, unity of action, he says [2] unity based upon the representation of a single person is artificial; the real unity of action consists in the plot being the representation of a single action : and to make the representation of this one action effective, the episodes must be, in the first place, pertinent, and, in the second, subordinate.

The effect produced by this excessive regard for the Aristotelian canons, real or imaginary, appears in the dramas of Corneille and Racine. 'Malgré les différences,' says Demogeot,[3] 'qui le [Racine] distinguent de son prédécesseur [Corneille], il y a entre eux une ressemblance que leur imposait leur époque. Tous deux sont spiritualistes au plus haut degré ; tous deux cherchent exclusivement dans la nature morale la source de leur puissance. Ils dédaignent ou ignorent le spectacle extérieur, le mouvement matériel de la scène, les couleurs toutes faites de l'histoire. Leurs tableaux ne sont pas des portraits, mais des types ; ce sont des idées qui ont pris sous leurs mains un corps et un visage. Ces poëtes n'embrassent point, comme Shakspeare, la réalité grossière pour l'élever à l'idéal ; ils saississent la pensée dans

[1] 1449[b].　　　　　　[2] 1451[a].
[3] *Histoire de la Littérature Française,* p. 413.

feigned history hath been to give some shadow of satisfaction
to the mind of man in those points wherein the nature of things
doth deny it; the world being in proportion inferior to the
soul; by reason whereof there is, agreeable to the spirit of man,
a more ample greatness, a more exact goodness, and a more
absolute variety, than can be found in the nature of things.
Therefore, because the acts and events of true history have
not that magnitude which satisfyeth the mind of man, poesy

son germe et l'échauffent sous leurs ailes jusqu'à ce qu'elle ait reçu
la vie.

'De là cette unité sévère, que subit Corneille et dont Racine porte
le joug si légèrement. De là ce petit nombre de personages, toujours
restreint aux indispensable besoins de l'intrigue; de là cette marche
rapide et non interrompue d'un seul et unique fait, de là enfin les
grands portiques déserts où se rencontrent les interlocuteurs, endroits
vagues, sans caractère et sans nom; où s'agite une action idéale dé-
pouillée avec soin de tout épisode vulgaire; en sorte qu'on peut dire
qu'il y a moins unité de temps et de lieur, que nullité de temps et de
lieur. L'action morale, spirituelle, semble vivre en elle-même, comme
la pensée, et n'occuper ni durée, ni espace.'

Concurrent with this study of Greek models was the effect produced
by the establishment of the Academy in 1637. Both of these influences
tended to produce a certain characteristic feeling of French thought
which Amiel notices.[1] 'The French lack that intuitive faculty to
which the living unity of things is revealed, they have very little sense
of what is sacred, very little penetration into the mysteries of being.
What they excel in is the construction of special sciences; the art of
writing a book, style, courtesy, grace, literary models, perfection and
urbanity; the spirit of order, the art of teaching, discipline, elegance,
truth of detail, power of arrangement; the desire and gift for pro-
selytism, the vigour necessary for practical couclusions. But if you
wish to travel in the *Inferno* or the *Paradiso* you must take other guides.'

With the recovery of French literature from the shock of the Revolution, and its revival at the beginning of the present century, there
came a broader and truer view of this doctrine of the unities, as well
as an expansion of the canons of art in general; and of this more
natural criticism we shall find hereafter a conspicuous exponent in
Victor Cousin.

---

[1] *Journal Intime*, translated by Mrs. Humphry Ward, p. 84.

feigneth acts and events greater and more heroical. Because history propoundeth the successes and issues of actions not so agreeable to the merits of virtue and vice, therefore poesy feigns them more just in retribution and more according to revealed providence.' [1]

Here we have a signal example of the power of learning to raise a man above the limitations of his own age, and project him into the future. The conception of poetry which is embodied in these words of Bacon is precisely that conception which has gained currency in the nineteenth century. It is a conception which recognises the existence in poetry of a separate order of thought, corresponding to the spiritual element in man ; and it is, therefore, an advance on the Greek conception, which had no room for spiritual aspirations. It is a conception, too, which sees in poetry a vehicle of thought which is capable of growing with the growth of man, and such a conception is alone consistent with the facts. For with the separation of the drama and the recognition of prose-fiction—a new form of creative literature which is independent of metre—structural perfection, beauty of form, is a less distinctive mark of poetic excellence ; on the other hand, with the development of man's moral nature, poetic thought has acquired an increased importance, for men have learnt that there is nowhere else in the whole region of literature, where these new aspirations can find such complete satisfaction as they find in the creations of the poet.

And it was in England, too, that the reconstruction commenced. For here, in the opening years of the eighteenth century, the first genuine critic appeared ;

[1] *Aavancement of Learning*, Book II. iv. 1, 2.

the first critic who formed a just conception of the duty of his office; the first critic who was able to add anything to the last word of Hellenism, by exhibiting the insufficiency of formal criticism and by establishing a new principle of poetic appeal.

Addison brought to the study of literature a mind which was open to receive impressions from every side. He commenced, as he was bound to do, with an application of the rules of Aristotle, but he acquired confidence in his own judgment as he proceeded in his researches, and finally availed himself freely of new elements of human knowledge which were unknown to Aristotle. His application of the Aristotelian canons to *Paradise Lost* was undertaken in deference to the spirit of the age, but in his essay on ' The Pleasures of the Imagination,' he discovers a new principle to which the charm and power of poetic literature is to be referred : a principle which, unlike the appeal to ' fear and pity,' is applicable not to one but to every form of poetry and fiction.   And in so doing he introduces fresh considerations, which affect all manifestations of art, but of which the rules of Aristotle take no account, and notices new effects for which these rules provide no tests ; and in supplying these omissions he has permanently widened the scope of criticism, whether the object of its inquiry be a picture or a poem, form or thought.

But before we proceed to examine the nature of this new principle of poetic appeal, which is Addison's chief contribution to the science of criticism, we have to consider the use which he made of Aristotle's treatise, and the developments which he introduced into the rules of the formal criticism of his age.

In the first place wé have to notice that he has formed a more enlightened conception of the duty of a critic of literature.

'Nothing is more absurd,' he says, 'than for a Man to set up for a Critick, without a good insight into all parts of learning. . . . One great Mark, by which you may discover a Critick, who has neither Taste nor Learning, is this, that he seldom ventures to praise any passage in an Author which has not been before received and applauded by the Public, and that his Criticism turns wholly upon little Faults and Errors. . . . A true Critick ought to dwell rather upon Excellences than Imperfections, to discover the concealed Beauties of a Writer, and communicate to the World such things as are worth their Observation. The most exquisite words and finest Strokes of an Author are those which very often appear the most doubtful and exceptionable to a man who wants a Relish for polite Learning ; and they are these which a sower undistinguished Critick generally attacks with the greatest Violence.' [1]

It was in this spirit of enlightened appreciation that he criticised the work of Milton ; and although he was compelled to descend to the level of the age, and apply the formal tests of the *Poetics* to *Paradise Lost*, yet by that application he vindicated once for all the claim of the Elizabethan and Stuart literature to a place in the hierarchy of genius. Moreover in his application of Aristotle's canons he offers no servile submission. On the contrary, where these rules have become obsolete owing to the development of poetry in its several forms, he is ready to point out their insufficiency. For example, in considering the 'characters' of *Paradise Lost*, he differs

[1] *Spectator*, 291.

in one particular from Aristotle, and he there states a principle which he applies with increasing confidence as he proceeds in his task.

'In this,' he writes, 'and some other very few Instances, Aristotle's Rules for Epic Poetry (which he had drawn from his reflections upon Homer) cannot be supposed to quadrate exactly with the Heroic Poems which have been made since his Time ; since it is plain his Rules would still have been more perfect, could he have perused the *Æneid* which was made some hundred years after his Death.' [1]

Again, with regard to the plot, he frankly admits that the form in which the change is from good to bad fortune —the form which is so strongly preferred by Aristotle for a tragedy, and by implication for an epic poem—is unsuitable for Epic, where, on the contrary, the principle of poetic justice should be exhibited.[2]

The general plan of his criticism of *Paradise Lost* is given at the close of the last [3] of the eighteen papers devoted to this subject. He assigns four papers to an examination of the poem under the separate heads of Fable, Characters, Sentiments, and Language ; two papers to the 'Censures which the author may incur under each of these heads'; and the remaining twelve to a consideration of each of the twelve books of the poem in turn, in which he points out 'particular beauties' and determines 'wherein they consist.'

This criticism presents two aspects. In the first place, it is an examination of Milton's work ; and in the next, it affords a commentary on Aristotle's treatise. In the present chapter I shall endeavour, first to gather up the

---

[1] Ib., 273.   [2] Ib., 297, and also 40.   [3] Ib., 369.

judgments pronounced upon the poem in the course of this application of the Aristotelian canons, and, secondly, to consider one or two passages which exhibit Addison most directly in the character of a commentator.

First, as to the verdict on *Paradise Lost*. Addison decides that *Paradise Lost* as a whole satisfies the requirements of the *Poetics* in respect of each of the four elements —Plot, Character, Sentiment, and Language—into which Aristotle resolves an epic poem. Milton, he says,[1] 'excels in general under each of these heads.' But this verdict of general approval is limited by the indication of particular deficiencies under each head.

The plot of *Paradise Lost* is deficient. In the first place, the 'event is unhappy'; and Addison holds that the final disaster, which is characteristic of the best form of tragedy, is not suitable for an epic poem.

'An Heroick Poem,' he writes,[2] 'according to the Opinion of the best Critics, ought to end happily, and leave the Mind of the Reader, after having conducted it through many Doubts and Fears, Sorrows and Disquietudes, in a State of Tranquillity and Satisfaction. Milton's Fable, which has so many other Qualifications to recommend it, is deficient in this Particular.'

But this defect, inherent in the nature of the subject, is partially remedied by Milton's genius.

'He leaves the Adversary of Mankind, in the last View which he gives us of him, under the lowest State of Mortification and Disappointment. We see him chewing Ashes, grovelling in the Dust, and loaden with Supernumerary Pains and Torments. On the contrary, our two first Parents are comforted by Dreams and Visions, cheared with Promises of

[1] Ib., 291.   [2] Ib., 369.

Salvation, and, in a manner, raised to a greater Happiness than that which they had forfeited : In short, Satan is represented as miserable in the height of his Triumphs, and Adam triumphant in the height of Misery.'

A second defect consists in the admission of particulars which are too improbable for an epic poem. Addison mentions the actions ascribed to *Sin* and *Death*, and the portrayal of the Limbo of Vanity and other passages in the Second Book. ' Such Allegories,' he remarks,[1] ' rather savour of the Spirit of Spencer and Ariosto, than of Homer and Virgil.' Also, the structure of the plot is deficient in so far as it contains too many digressions. ' Digressions are by no means to be allowed of in an Epic Poem. If the Poet, even in the ordinary course of his Narration, should speak as little as possible, he should certainly never let his Narration sleep for the sake of any Reflections of his own.' The instances which Addison gives[2] are, Milton's complaint for his blindness, his panegyric on marriage, his reflections on Adam and Eve going naked, and on the angels eating. But his condemnation of these and other similar passages is limited by the remark, ' tho' I must confess there is so great a Beauty in these very Digressions, that I would not wish them out of the Poem.'

The defect which Addison finds in Milton's characters consists in the introduction of ' two actors of a shadowy and fictitious nature, in the persons of *Sin* and *Death*.' He attributes this defect to the fact that the subject itself was naturally limited in this respect, and to the desire of the poet to introduce as much variety as possible into his creations. The human characters were limited by the

[1] Ib., 297.   [2] Ib.

subject to Adam and Eve. Satan was the 'principal actor' in the poem, and in this and the other divine persons introduced by Milton, Addison sees as much substantiality as in Homer's gods and heroes. But he objects [1] to these allegorical characters, because 'there is not that measure of probability annexed to them, which is requisite in writings of this kind.' In a subsequent passage he explains more fully the grounds upon which his objection is based. And in this fuller criticism [2] it is worthy of note that Addison anticipates a good deal of what was afterwards said by Lessing with greater definiteness in the *Laocoon*. What is there represented as a question to be decided by the consideration of the respective methods of poetry and painting, is here discussed by Addison with reference only to a single form of poetry. These shadowy and imaginary persons, he says, if introduced into an Epic, or narrative poem, should not be described and made to take part in the action, but merely *suggested* in the manner of Homer and Virgil.

'I shall beg leave,' he says, 'to explain myself in a Matter which is curious in its Kind, and which none of the Criticks have treated of. It is certain Homer and Virgil are full of imaginary Persons, who are very beautiful in Poetry where they are just shewn, without being engaged in any Series of Actions. Homer indeed represents Sleep as a Person, and ascribes a short Part to him in his *Iliad*, but we must consider that tho' we now regard such a Person as entirely shadowy and unsubstantial, the Heathens made Statues of him, placed him in their Temples, and looked upon him as a real Deity. When Homer makes use of other such Allegorical Persons, it is only in short Expressions, which convey

[1] Ib., 273.   [2] Ib., 357.

an ordinary Thought to the Mind in the most pleasing manner, and may rather be looked upon as Poetical Phrases than Allegorical Descriptions. Instead of telling us that Men naturally fly when they are terrified, he introduces the Persons of Flight and Fear, who, he tells us, are inseparable Companions. Instead of saying that the time was come when Apollo ought to have received his Recompence, he tells us, that the Hours brought him his Reward. . . . Milton has likewise very often made use of the same way of Speaking, as when he tells us, that Victory sat on the Right Hand of the Messiah. . . . But when such Persons are introduced as principal Actors, and engaged in a series of Adventures, they take too much upon them, and are by no means proper for an Heroick Poem, which ought to appear credible in its principal Parts.'

Addison finds three defects in Milton's 'Sentiments.' They are 'too much pointed,' and even 'degenerate into puns'; the 'frequent allusion to Heathen Fables' is incongruous, considering the subject-matter of the poem; and there is an 'unnecessary ostentation of learning' appearing in his dissertations on 'Free-Will and Predestination, and his many glances upon History, Astronomy, Geography and the like.' And he condemns his 'Language' on almost similar grounds. It is obscured by the use of 'old words, transpositions, and foreign idioms'; 'a kind of jingle in his words' is apparent in such passages as these :

> ' And brought into the *world* a *world* of woe.
>   —Begirt th' Almighty throne
>   *Beseeching* or *besieging*—
>   This *tempted* our *attempt*—
> At one slight *bound* high overleapt all *bound*.'

And there is a frequent use of technical terms ; whereas
' it is one of the great beauties of poetry to make hard
things intelligible, and to deliver what is abstruse of itself
in such easy language as may be understood of ordinary
readers.'[1]

Having indicated these blemishes (which he compares
to the spots in the sun), Addison proceeds to the more
congenial task of pointing out those beauties in Milton's
poem which appear ' more exquisite than the rest.'   This
appreciation of *Paradise Lost* occupies twice as much
space as the preceding criticism ; but it is impossible
here to do more than refer to one or two of the more
conspicuous conclusions.   It may, however, be remarked
in passing, that of the many passages which Addison
quotes, there are very few which do not appeal to the
modern critic.

He early decides that Satan is the principal character
of the poem, and in his appreciation he notices[2] the
conspicuous beauty of the scenes and speeches in which
the Miltonic Satan is presented to our minds.

> ' He above the rest
> In shape and gesture proudly eminent
> Stood like a tower.'

He has already[3] decided, too, that sublimity is the
characteristic excellence of Milton's poetry :

' Milton's chief Talent, and indeed his distinguishing Excellence, lies in the Sublimity of his Thoughts.   There are
others of the Moderns who rival him in every other Part of
Poetry ; but in the greatness of his Sentiments he triumphs over
all the Poets, both modern and ancient, Homer only excepted.

Ib., 297.   [2] Ib., 303.   [3] Ib., 279.

It is impossible for the Imagination of Man to distend itself with greater Ideas, than those which he has laid together in his First, Second, and Sixth Books.'

And in this appreciation he illustrates with special fulness the culminating splendours of the Battle of the Angels in the Sixth Book, down to the moment when, under the wheels of the chariot of the Messiah,

> 'The steadfast Empyrean shook throughout,
> All but the throne itself of God.'

He also selects and illustrates with scarcely less detail those scenes in which Milton has succeeded in achieving another special excellence of epic poetry, the happy blending of the marvellous and the probable.

'If the Fable is only Probable, it differs nothing from a true History ; if it is only Marvellous, it is no better than a Romance. The great Secret therefore of Heroic Poetry is to relate such Circumstances, as may produce in the Reader at the same time both Belief and Astonishment. This is brought to pass in a well-chosen Fable, by the Account of such things as have really happened, or at least of such things as have happened according to the received Opinions of Mankind. Milton's Fable is a Masterpiece of this Nature ; as the War in Heaven, the Condition of the fallen Angels, the State of Innocence, and Temptation of the Serpent, and the Fall of Man, though they are very astonishing in themselves, are not only credible, but actual Points of Faith.' [1]

But one of the objects which Addison tells us he had in view in this application of Aristotle's rules to *Paradise Lost*, was to furnish a commentary on the *Poetics*. In one sense it is as much a criticism of Aristotle as of

[1] Ib., 315.

Milton ; since the deficiencies of the critic's theory are exhibited as well as the deficiencies of the poet's practice.

Considered as a commentary, Addison's remarks are in general conspicuous for their good sense and elegance ; and in two important particulars he extends Aristotle's principles. In discussing the theory of the plot he introduces the consideration of ' poetical justice,' and he widens the significance of ' sentiment ' and ' language ' as elements of poetic composition. These are points which will be more fully discussed in the two following chapters ; but apart from this he sometimes applies himself to special passages in the *Poetics*, and these special passages he treats no less successfully than the general theory. I propose to bring this chapter to a close with one or two of these comments.

We will take the difficult passage in which Aristotle explains the quality of ' magnitude,' as requisite to the action on which a tragedy is based.

' Since beauty,' he says,[1] ' whether in a living creature or anything else which is composed of parts, requires not merely the due proportion of the parts, but in the first instance an appropriate magnitude in the whole—for beauty consists in a union of magnitude and proportion ; and, therefore, neither can anything excessively small be a beautiful creature, because nothing but a confused whole is seen where the perception is almost instantaneous ; nor anything excessively large, for it is not enough to look once, but the sight has lost unity and wholeness for the spectator, for example, in the case of an animal a thousand miles long—it follows that just as in the case of human bodies and animals there should be magnitude, but magnitude which can be readily traversed by the eye, so too in the case of plots,

[1] 1450b–1451a.

while there must be length, it must be such length as can be readily kept in the mind.'

On this passage Addison's comment is elegant and luminous.[1]

'Aristotle, by the Greatness of the Action, does not only mean that it should be great in its nature, but also in its Duration, or in other words that it should have a due Length in it, as well as what we properly call Greatness. The just Measure of this kind of Magnitude, he explains by the following Similitude. An animal no bigger than a Mite cannot appear perfect to the Eye, because the Sight takes it in at once, and has only a confused Idea of the Whole, and not a distinct Idea of all its Parts; if on the contrary you should suppose an Animal of ten thousand Furlongs in length, the Eye would be so filled with a single Part of it, that it could not give the Mind an Idea of the Whole. What these Animals are to the Eye, a very short or a very long Action would be to the Memory. The first would be, as it were, lost and swallowed up by it, and the other difficult to be contained in it. Homer and Virgil have shown their principal Art in this Particular; the Action of the *Iliad*, and that of the *Æneid*, were in themselves exceeding short, but are so beautifully extended and diversified by the Invention of Episodes, and the Machinery of Gods, with the like poetical Ornaments, that they make up an agreeable Story, sufficient to employ the Memory without overcharging it. Milton's action is enriched with such a Variety of Circumstances, that I have taken as much pleasure in reading the Contents of his Books, as in the best invented Story I ever met with.'

Again, in speaking of Epic, Aristotle says,[2] that 'among the many reasons we have for admiring Homer, none is stronger than the fact that he is the only poet who

[1] *Spectator*, 267.   [2] 1460a.

knows his business.' He then enunciates a general principle :

' The poet ought himself to say very little : for when he does he is not an imitator. Other poets strive to appear in their own persons throughout, while they imitate little and seldom. But Homer, after a few words of prelude, at once leads on a man or a woman, or some other character, introducing no person without character, but always a characterisation.'

On this Addison remarks : [1]

' It is finely observed by Aristotle, that the author of an Heroick Poem should seldom speak himself, but throw as much of his Work as he can into the Mouths of those who are his Principal Actors.' He proceeds, ' Aristotle has given no reason for this precept ; but I presume it is because the Mind of the Reader is more awed and elevated when he hears Æneas or Achilles speak, than when Virgil or Homer talk in their own Persons. Besides that assuming the character of an eminent Man, is apt to fire the Imagination and raise the Ideas of the Author.'

Here, at first sight, Addison appears to have been guilty of an omission ; for the *Poetics* give a reason, namely, that the poet when he speaks in his own person ' is no longer an imitator.' But this reason after all only amounts to a statement that an Epic poem should be thrown as much as possible into a dramatic form. It does not explain why this should be so. Addison gives two reasons, both of which are pertinent. The change from the third to the first person suggests the actual presence of the character represented to the mind of the reader—it is Æneas, not Virgil, who speaks. And in the second place, the author's realisation of the character

[1] *Spectator*, 297.

becomes more intense. That is to say, he adopts the principle which Aristotle himself advises in another part of the *Poetics*, where the dramatic artist is told to visualise the scenes in constructing his plot.[1]

One more instance. Under the head of 'diction' Aristotle says: 'The diction should be elaborated in the idle parts of the poem which do not reveal either character or sentiment : for an over-brilliant diction obscures instead of heightening the effect produced by both character and sentiment.'[2]

Addison points out[3] how Milton has applied the principle in his description of Paradise :

'In the Description of Paradise, the Poet has observed Aristotle's Rule of lavishing all the Ornaments of Diction on the weak unactive Parts of the Fable, which are not supported by the Beauty of Sentiments and Characters. Accordingly the Reader may observe that the Expressions are more florid and elaborate in these Descriptions than in most other Parts of the Poem. I must further add that tho' the Drawings of Gardens, Rivers, Rainbows, and the like Dead Pieces of Nature, are justly censured in an Heroick Poem, when they run out into an unnecessary length; the Description of Paradise would have been faulty, had not the Poet been very particular in it, not only as it is the Scene of the Principal Action, but as it is requisite to give us an Idea of that Happiness from which our first Parents fell.'

[1] 1455ᵃ. [2] 1460ᵇ. [3] *Spectator*, 321.

CHAPTER IV

In the *Poetics* Aristotle insists upon the importance of the plot as the supreme element in tragedy. The doctrine is enforced in two ways : first, by a general application of the philosophic doctrine of the 'final aim' ($\tau\acute{\epsilon}\lambda o\varsigma$) ; and secondly, by a reference to the nature of the final aim of that human life of which tragedy is a representation. Just as the sum of effort in man has a final aim or purpose— well-being or happiness—to which all particular effort is subservient, so tragedy has a final aim—the representation of human action—to which all lesser aims must be subordinated. Again, the facts of life tell us that from this standpoint of happiness, men are measured not by their capacity to act, but by the acts which they have performed—*factis non verbis*. In the delineation of character there is only a promise of action ; the plot is itself the representation of action, and therefore the performance of that which is the final aim of tragedy. And so while the plot is 'the central principle and soul, so to speak, of tragedy, character is second in importance ?'[1] It is the feeling which produced this doctrine—or rather which produced the forms of poetic composition upon which the doctrine is itself based—which, according to Matthew

[1] 1450ª (and *passim*).

Arnold, makes the difference between Greek and modern poetry.

'The radical difference,' he writes,[1] 'between their poetical theory and ours consists, as it appears to me, in this : that, with them, the poetical character of an action in itself and the conduct of it was the first consideration ; with us attention is fixed mainly on the value of the separate thoughts and images which occur in the treatment of an action.   They regarded the whole ; we regard the parts.'

I have already suggested [2] that the overwhelming importance assigned to the plot in Aristotle's theory of poetry is to be referred to another cause—namely, that he has neglected to distinguish between the importance of the plot as an element of tragedy, and its importance as an element of poetic composition in general.   If this suggestion be correct—if, that is to say, Aristotle has applied to other forms of poetry a principle which is only applicable to tragedy ; and if, further, we had a criticism of Epic and other forms of Greek poetry as full as Aristotle's criticism of tragedy, we should then find that the attention of the Greeks was in the case of these other poems directed to the 'separate thoughts and images which occur in the treatment of an action.'   In short we must look for some deeper principle than any which arises out of a mere critical theory if we would realise the difference between the Greek and modern conception of poetry. At the same time, we first get a clue to the nature of this difference by noticing the test for the construction of the plot which Aristotle gives ; for this test is also a test by which the scope and purpose of the poetic representation

---

[1] *Irish Essays*, p. 288.   [2] Chapter ii. p. 46.

of the facts of life can be measured. When Aristotle decides that the most perfect form of plot for a tragedy is that which ends in a disaster, and when he applies this, by implication at least, to the plot of an Epic, it is evident that the conception of poetry to which he gives expression is one which is essentially different from that which obtains in our own age. For the basis of the modern conception is the doctrine of ' poetical justice ' as enunciated in the passage from Bacon which has already been quoted.[1]

In order to contrast this doctrine of ' poetical justice ' with Aristotle's treatment of the plot in tragedy, we must return to the *Poetics* and glance at the different forms of plot which are there distinguished.

In the course of this discussion three main kinds of plots are distinguished. In the first place we have [2] the division of plots into simple ($\dot{a}\pi\lambda o\hat{\iota}$) and complicated ($\pi\epsilon\pi\lambda\epsilon\gamma\mu\epsilon\nu o\iota$). The characteristic of the latter is the introduction of a ' revolution ' or a ' recognition,' or of both. In the second place, we have [3] the division into ' single ' ($\dot{a}\pi\lambda o\hat{\upsilon}s$) and ' double ' ($\delta\iota\pi\lambda o\hat{\upsilon}s$) applied to the second of the two first-mentioned kinds, the ' complicated.' In the single-complicated plot the hero passes from good to bad fortune ; in the double-complicated, he passes first from good to bad, and then again from bad to good fortune. Aristotle decides [4] that the plot of a tragedy, and by inference the plot of an epic poem, should be of the nature of the single-complicated ; that is to say, that it should be so constructed that the fortunes of the hero should change through revolution and recognition

---

[1] P. 49.   [2] 1452[a].
[3] 1453[a].   [4] Ib. and 1459[a].

from good to bad, ending when the tragic interest is highest in the disaster.

Now Addison adopts the rule of Aristotle as regards tragedy, but he decides that it does not apply to Epic; and in giving his reasons for this opinion he discusses the whole question of poetic justice.

'The English writers of Tragedy,' he writes,[1] 'are possessed with a Notion that when they represent a virtuous or innocent Person in Distress, they ought not to leave him till they have delivered him out of his Troubles, or made him triumph over his Enemies. This Error they have been led into by a ridiculous Doctrine in modern Criticism, that they are obliged to an equal Distribution of Rewards and Punishments, and an impartial Execution of Poetical Justice. Who were the first that established this Rule I know not; but I am sure it has no Foundation in Nature, in Reason, or in the Practice of the Ancients. We find that Good and Evil happen alike to all men on this side the Grave; and as the principal Design of Tragedy is to raise Commiseration and Terror in the Minds of the Audience, we shall defeat this great End, if we always make Virtue and Innocence happy and successful. Whatever Crosses and Disappointments a good man suffers in the Body of the Tragedy, they will make but small Impression on our Minds, when we know that in the last Act he is to arrive at the End of his Wishes and Desires. When we see him engaged in the Depth of his Afflictions, we are apt to comfort ourselves, because we are sure he will find his Way out of them: and that his Grief, how great soever it may be at present, will soon terminate in Gladness. For this Reason the ancient Writers of Tragedy treated Men in their Plays, as they are dealt with in the World, by making Virtue sometimes happy and sometimes miserable, as they found it in the Fable which they made choice of, or as it might affect their Audience in the most agreeable Manner.

[1] *Spectator*, 40.

Aristotle considers the Tragedies that were written in either of these Kinds, and observes, That those which ended unhappily had always pleased the People and carried away the Prize in the Public Disputes of the Stage, from those that ended happily.[1] Terror and Commiseration leave a pleasing Anguish in the Mind ; and fix the Audience in such a serious Composure of Thought as is much more lasting and delightful than any little transient Starts of Joy and Satisfaction. Accordingly, we find that more of our English Tragedies have succeeded, in which the Favourites of the Audience sink under their Calamities, than those in which they recover themselves out of them. The best Plays of this kind are *The Orphan, Venice Preserved, Alexander the Great, Theodosius, All for Love, Œdipus, Oroonoko, Othello,* &c. *King Lear* is an admirable Tragedy of the same kind, as Shakespear wrote it ; but as it is reformed according to the chimerical Notion of Poetical Justice, in my humble Opinion, it has lost half its Beauty. At the same time I must allow that there are very noble Tragedies which have been framed upon the other Plan, and have ended happily ; as, indeed, most of the good Tragedies, which have been written since the starting of the above-mentioned Criticism, have taken this Turn : As *The Mourning Bride, Tamerlane, Ulysses, Phaedra and Hippolitus,* with most of Mr. Dryden's. I must also allow that many of Shakespear's, and several of the celebrated Tragedies of Antiquity, are cast in the same Form. I do not, therefore, dispute against this Way of writing Tragedies, but against the Criticism that would establish this as the only Method ; and by that means would very much cramp the English Tragedy, and perhaps give a wrong Bent to the Genius of our Writers.'

[1] This is not quite what Aristotle says. He says (*Poetics*, 1453ᵃ), speaking of Euripides, that the change from good to bad fortune is right ; ' tragedies so constructed have a most tragic effect—if they are otherwise successful ; and Euripides, whatever faults may be otherwise found with his method, appears to be the most tragic of poets.'

To this must be added a passage which occurs in the criticism of the plot of *Paradise Lost.*[1]

'The most taking Tragedies among the Ancients were built on this last sort of Implex Fable [*i.e.* the single-complicated], particularly the Tragedy of Oedipus, which proceeds upon a Story, if we may believe Aristotle, the most proper for Tragedy that could be invented by the Wit of Man. I have taken some Pains in a former Paper to show that this kind of Implex Fable, wherein the Event is unhappy, is more apt to affect an Audience than that of the first kind : notwithstanding many excellent Pieces among the Ancients, as well as most of those which have been written of late Years in our own Country, are raised upon contrary Plans. I must, however, own that I think this kind of Fable, which is the most perfect in Tragedy, is not so proper for an Heroick Poem.'

It appears, therefore, that Aristotle's rule (within the limits stated in the *Poetics*) cannot be controverted as regards the construction of a tragedy ; but that a distinction must be made between tragedy and other fictions, whether in verse or prose. Both a narrative poem and a novel give a general picture of life, and to say that human action is most truly represented as ending in disaster is to force the poet into pronouncing a criticism of life which is by no means universally true. Such a criticism is admitted to be repugnant to popular sentiment even in tragedy. The apparent superiority of the plot which ends happily, says Aristotle,[2] 'is due to a deficiency in public taste,' and the poets construct such plots because they give pleasure (but not the *right* pleasure) to the audience. And Addison speaks of the belief that the poets 'are obliged to an equal distribution of rewards

---

[1] *Spectator,* 297.　　　　　[2] 1453ᵃ.

and punishments,' though he characterises it as a 'ridiculous doctrine.' Similarly the modern novel reader
expects a 'happy ending.'

Now truth in art is different from truth in nature, and
the question cannot be decided, therefore, solely by an
appeal to the facts of life ; assuming, that is to say, that
this appeal showed a balance on the side of unhappiness.
At the same time the theory of poetic justice, as an
artistic doctrine, can be maintained both on philosophic
and technical grounds. The philosophic basis is contained in that passage of Bacon to which I have already
referred,[1] as presenting what is essentially the modern
conception of poetry. The use of Feigned History, or
Poetry, Bacon says, is ' to give some shadow of satisfaction to the mind of man in those points wherein the
nature of things doth deny it.' I now add the con-
cluding sentences : [2]

' Because true history representeth actions and events more
ordinary and less interchanged, therefore poesy endueth them
with more rareness, and more unexpected and alternative variations. So as it appeareth that poesy serveth and conferreth to
magnanimity, morality, and to delectation. And therefore it
was ever thought to have some participation of divineness,
because it doth raise and erect the mind by submitting the
shows of things to the desires of the mind, whereas reason doth
buckle and bow the mind into the nature of things. And we
see that by these insinuations and congruities with man's nature
and pleasure, joined also with the agreement and consort it hath
with music, it hath had access and estimation in rude times and
barbarous regions, where other learning stood excluded.'

[1] Chapter iii. p. 49.
[2] *Advancement of Learning*, Bk. II. iv. s. 2.

The technical basis lies in the universal recognition now assigned to the idealising function of art. The idealising process, which forms part of the art of poetry, must be applied to action and life as a whole, as well as to character and individual action. Beauty in poetry, as in the other fine arts, depends in the first place on the selection of materials in Nature. When Addison writes of the pleasures of the imagination, he recognises the truth of this principle of poetic justice in its broader aspect, though he has denied it when it seemed inconsistent with Aristotle's rule for the plot of a tragedy. Here [1] he writes : 'It is the part of a poet to humour the imagination in its own notions, by mending and perfecting Nature where he describes a reality, and by adding greater beauties than are put together in Nature where he describes a fiction.' This statement of the principle of selection in poetry cannot be reconciled with what he has said before.[2] 'For this reason the ancient writers of Tragedy treated men in their plays, *as they are dealt with in the world. . . .*' It is impossible for the artist to do this. The justification for the unhappy ending in tragedy lies in the fact that a tragedy is a specific form of poetry which has for its object to raise the emotions of fear and pity. This point has been excellently worked out in Mr. Moulton's studies of Shakespeare's plays. Poetic justice, he says,[3] does not only mean 'the correction of justice,' but, more truly, it is to be regarded as 'the modification of justice by considerations of art.' And he explains how this modification is applied in the case of the drama.

[1] *Spectator*, 418—'Pleasures of the Imagination.'
[2] See p. 68.   [3] *Shakespeare as a Dramatic Artist*, p. 300.

' The Drama does with human experience what Painting does with external nature. There are landscapes whose beauty is obvious to all ; but it is one of the privileges of the artist to reveal the charm that lies in the most ordinary scenery, until the ideal can be recognised everywhere, and nature itself becomes lost. Similarly there are striking points in life, such as the vindication of justice, which all can catch ; but it is for the dramatist, as the artist in life, to arrange the experience he depicts so as to bring out the hidden beauties of fate until the trained eye sees a meaning in all that happens ; until indeed the word " suffering " itself has only to be translated into its Greek equivalent, and *pathos* is recognised as a form of beauty. Accumulating pathos then must be added to Poetic Justice as a determinant of fate in the Drama.'

But in other forms of poetic art this ' accumulation of pathos ' is not required : and in these forms, where the purpose of the poet is no longer mainly to raise the emotions of ' pity and fear,' the common sentiment of mankind, which requires poetry ' to feign events more just in retribution,' can be legitimately satisfied, or rather, this satisfaction is a necessary part of the idealising function of art. It is ' a modification of justice by considerations of art.'

The doctrine of poetic justice appears in a still more definite form in the expectation of the reader for a ' moral ' in a work of fiction. This expectation can be most easily and legitimately satisfied in prose fiction, and I shall hereafter suggest that it forms an appreciable element in the modern novel regarded as a form of literature. It is interesting, therefore, in view of the subsequent development of this element in fiction, to notice what Addison says of the moral of an epic poem.

Commenting upon the opinion of René le Bossu,[1] he remarks : [2]

'Though I can by no means think, with the last-mentioned French Author, that an Epick Writer first of all pitches upon a certain Moral, as the Ground-work and Foundation of his Poem, and afterwards finds out a story to it : I am however of opinion that no just Heroick Poem ever was or can be made, from whence one great Moral may not be deduced. That which reigns in Milton is the most useful and the most universal that can be imagined ; it is in short this, *That Obedience to the will of God makes Men happy, and that Disobedience makes them miserable.*'

And to round off the discussion we may note Addison's account of the nature and effects of the tragic appeal to the emotions, and his perception of the development of the drama.

'As a perfect Tragedy is the Noblest Production of Human Nature, so it is capable of giving the Mind one of the most delightful and most improving Entertainments. A Virtuous Man (says Seneca) struggling with Misfortunes, is such a Spectacle as Gods might look upon with Pleasure : And such a Pleasure it is which one meets with in the Representation of a well-written Tragedy. Diversions of this kind wear out of our Thoughts everything that is mean and little. They cherish and cultivate that Humanity which is the Ornament of our Nature. They soften Insolence, soothe Affliction, and subdue the Mind to the Dispensations of Providence. . . .

'The modern Tragedy excels that of Greece and Rome, in the Intricacy and Disposition of the Fable ; but, what a Christian Writer would be ashamed to own, falls infinitely short of it in the Moral Part of the Performance.' [3]

[1] *Treatise on the Epic*, in 1675.   [2] *Spectator*, 379.   [3] Ib., 39.

In this passage the influence of the Aristotelian system is predominant. But I add an opinion subsequently written on the structure of Shakespeare's plays. This opinion occurs in the later criticism, when Addison's study of psychology had given him a truer conception of the artistic basis of poetry.

'Our Inimitable Shakespear is a Stumbling-Block to the whole Tribe of these rigid Criticks. Who would not rather read one of his Plays, where there is not a single Rule of the Stage observed, than any production of a Modern Critick, where there is not one of them violated? Shakespear was indeed born with all the Seeds of Poetry, and may be compared to the Stone in Pyrrhus's Ring, which, as Pliny tells us, had the Figure of Apollo and the Nine Muses in the Veins of it, produced by the spontaneous Hand of Nature, without any Help from Art.'[1]

What Addison has here written of Shakespeare is true of his own writings. His papers contain 'all the seeds of criticism'—seeds which have grown since into well-developed plants. And, in order to render this brief survey of his researches more comprehensive, I propose now to lay before the reader certain extracts which contain what is most definite in his opinions on some aspects of literature which lie outside the strict limits of formal criticism.

In the first place, Addison gives a clear verdict on a question which has occupied a large space in the works of contemporary writers on art—the question of the ultimate test of merit in a work of art. The passage arises out of a discussion of a point of musical criticism. Addison maintains in this discussion that the difference

[1] Ib., 592.

between the Italian and English language requires a corresponding difference in the style of musical composition. 'An English composer,' he says,[1] 'should not follow the Italian Recitative too servilely, but make use of many gentle deviations from it, in compliance with his own native language.' He then enunciates the principle upon which this opinion is based, and subsequently extends this principle to the other arts, deciding that 'taste' and not 'the rules of the special art' is the ultimate test of merit in all alike.

'A Composer should fit his Musick to the Genius of the People, and consider that the Delicacy of Hearing, and Taste of Harmony, has been formed upon those Sounds which every Country abounds with: In short, that Musick is of a Relative Nature, and what is Harmony to one Ear, may be Dissonance to another.'

'I shall add no more to what I have here offered, than that Musick, Architecture, and Painting, as well as Poetry and Oratory, are to deduce their Laws and Rules from the general Sense and Taste of Mankind, and not from the Principles of those Arts themselves; or, in other words, the Taste is not to conform to the Art, but the Art to the Taste. Musick is not designed to please only Chromatick Ears, but all that are Capable of distinguishing harsh from disagreeable Notes. A man of an Ordinary Ear is a Judge whether a Passion is expressed in proper Sounds, and whether the Melody of those Sounds be more or less pleasing.'

Again, the interpretation of Nature has become a recognised object of poetic thought. In the following passage[2] Addison indicates the philosophic basis upon which the artistic value of the poetic treatment of external Nature depends.

[1] Ib., 29.   [2] Ib., 293.

'Natural Philosophy quickens this Taste of the Creation, and renders it not only pleasing to the Imagination, but to the Understanding. It does not rest in the Murmur of Brooks, and the Melody of Birds, in the Shade of Groves and Woods, or in the Embroidery of Fields and Meadows, but considers the several Ends of Providence which are served by them, and the Wonders of Divine Wisdom which appear in them. It heightens the Pleasures of the Eye, and raises such a rational Admiration in the Soul as is little inferior to Devotion.'

As we shall hereafter have occasion to notice, the poetry of Wordsworth (to take the most prominent example) owes its charm not to a reproduction of the sensible aspects of Nature, but to the reproduction of the spiritual principles suggested to the mind by these sensible beauties.

Further, we may suitably include among these 'opinions' of Addison the set of papers which contain an examination of the various manifestations of the ludicrous.

Addison's account of Humour and Wit is mainly negative. He gives us a series of examples of false humour and false wit, and then, after this preparatory discussion, states briefly the principles upon which the legitimate manifestations of both depend.

His positive account of Humour is contained in an allegorical statement [1] of the respective parentage of False and True Humour. False humour, the impostor, is the child of Frenzy and Laughter ; Laughter is a daughter of Folly, and Frenzy is the son of Nonsense, the daughter of Falsehood. Humour is the youngest of an illustrious family ; his parents were Wit and Mirth, and his ancestors Good-sense and Truth. Humour, then, according

[1] Ib., 35.

to Addison, is Wit with an element of Mirth super-
added ; and it becomes necessary, in order to know the
character of Humour, to first acquire a knowledge of the
nature of Wit. For the present, therefore, he contents
himself with a list of the characteristics of False Humour.
False Humour is 'exceedingly given to little apish tricks
and buffooneries ;' he delights in mimicry so much that
it is 'all one to him whether he exposes by it Vice and
Folly, Luxury and Avarice ; or, on the contrary, Virtue
and Wisdom, Pain and Poverty ;' he ridicules both
friends and foes alike ; he 'pursues no point either of
morality or instruction, but is ludicrous only for the
sake of being so ;' and lastly, 'being incapable of anything but mock representations, his ridicule is always
personal, and aimed at the Vicious Man, or the Writer ;
not at the Vice, or the writing.'

As Humour is mirthful Wit, Addison's account of Wit
is naturally more complete.[1] He gives us a long list of
the various forms of false wit, classical, mediæval, and
contemporary, with appropriate examples of 'scholar's
eggs,' anagrams, rebuses, *bouts-rimez*, and other absurd
conceits down to the ordinary pun. With respect to this
latter, he decides that the test by which a 'piece of wit'
may be distinguished from a mere pun is the test of translation into another language. As an example he takes
Aristinetus's description of a fine woman : 'When she
is dressed she is beautiful, when she is undressed she is
beautiful ;' which bears the translation, *Induitur, formosa
est : exuitur, ipsa forma est.*

In his positive account of Wit he first distinguishes
between 'wit' and 'judgment.' Following Locke,[2] whom

1 Ib., 58–63.   2 Ib., 62.

he quotes, he decides that wit is characterised by the perception of affinities, ' the assemblage of Ideas ;' whereas judgment depends upon analysis, the separation of ideas which have an apparent likeness. And he points out the obvious deficiency of Dryden's definition ; 'a propriety of words and thoughts adapted to the subject.' He has already discovered, in commenting[1] upon Hobbes's account of laughter, that the basis of our perception of the ludicrous is a sense of our own superiority suddenly awakened by our being confronted with inferiority in others. This, together with Locke's analysis, enables him to recognise in ' comparison ' and ' surprise ' the two primary elements of Wit.

' Every Resemblance of Ideas is not that which we call Wit, unless it be such an one that gives Delight and Surprise to the Reader : These two properties seem essential to Wit, more particularly the last of them. In order, therefore, that the Resemblance in the Ideas be Wit, it is necessary that the Ideas should not lie too near to one another in the Nature of things ; for where the Likeness is obvious it gives no Surprise. . . . Thus when the Poet tells us that the Bosom of his Mistress is as white as Snow, there is no Wit in the Comparison ; but when he adds, with a Sigh, that it is as cold too, it then grows into Wit.' [2]

To this he adds two remarks which are both pregnant. True wit consists in the resemblance of *ideas*, false wit in the resemblance of the mere symbols of ideas, words, syllables, and even letters. And, on the other hand, an opposition of ideas may have the same effect as a resemblance of ideas, for in such cases the opposition implies or suggests the unexpressed resemblance.

[1] Ib., 47.   [2] Ib., 62.

As it is not intended to return to the theory of humour in any subsequent chapter, I may be allowed to add here a passage from Emerson which seems to me to carry the discussion a step farther. Aristotle, it will be remembered, tells us in the *Poetics*[1] that 'the sense of the ridiculous arises from our perception of a defect, a painless and harmless depravity, moral or physical.' His meaning is made plainer by the example which is given. It is the comic mask, which is 'a deformed and perverted object which can be looked upon without pain.'[2] This idea of a departure from a standard of physical or moral rightness too insignificant to involve an appeal to our conscience or our humanity is embodied and expanded in Emerson's essay on 'The Comic.' 'The essence of all jokes, of all comedy, is the non-performance of what is pretended to be performed.' He then proceeds :

'The presence of the ideal of right and of truth in all action makes the yawning delinquencies of practice remorseful to the conscience, tragic to the interest, but droll to the intellect. The activity of our sympathies may for a time hinder our perceiving the fact intellectually, and so deriving mirth from it ; but all falsehoods, all vices seen at sufficient distance, seen from the point where our moral sympathies do not interfere, become ludicrous. The comedy is the intellect's perception of discrepancy.'

These extracts make both the nature of the subject of humour and the cause of our enjoyment plain. The physical or moral depravity which is the subject of humour must not cause us pain either by appealing to our humanity or by outraging our sense of decorum ; to do either will

[1] 1449ᵃ.   [2] αἰσχρόν τι καὶ διεστραμμένον ἄνευ ὀδύνης.

prevent us from making the comparison necessary for our perception of the defect in the light of the ideal. The extent of our enjoyment depends upon the degree in which we are able (or think we are able) to identify ourselves with this ideal. If we add to this the thought that comedy is humour in its literary form, we shall arrive at a tolerably correct conclusion of the nature of both.

CHAPTER V

ADDISON'S TREATMENT OF THE IMAGINATION AS A
SEPARATE FACULTY OF THE MIND INTRODUCES A
NEW PRINCIPLE INTO CRITICISM

BUT it is in the 'Essay on the Pleasures of the Imagination' that Addison's real theory of creative literature
appears. The distinction between his theory and Aristotle's can be stated in a single sentence. Aristotle
found that the plot was the 'central principle and soul'
of tragedy ; Addison finds that the 'talent of affecting
the Imagination' is the 'very life and highest perfection'
of poetry. A brief consideration of these two statements
will reveal the principles which respectively underlie them.

The plot was the soul of tragedy, because it was only
by a skilful arrangement of the incidents that a powerful
appeal to the emotions of fear and pity could be produced.
But the appeal to the emotions, the element of pathos,
which is so conspicuous and valuable in tragedy is not
equally conspicuous and valuable in other forms of poetry.
Addison, therefore, noticing this, was compelled to seek
for a new principle wide enough to cover the appeal, not
only of tragedy, but of all poetry and fiction. Why
should certain incidents, when arranged by the poet, affect
us more powerfully than the same incidents, or the same
class of incidents, in real life ? Further, why should the
description of actions and objects, which are in themselves

disagreeable, affect us pleasurably when presented by the poet ? The answer is, that just as the raw material of human action is endowed with a mental value by being combined into a plot, so individual actions and single events, and even visible and tangible objects when they are selected for representation, are subject to a transformation process in the mind of the artist ; and it is only when they have been so transformed that they are presented to us by poetry and the arts. When so presented they affect our minds in a different manner, and in different degrees, from the manner, or degrees, in which they would affect us if they reached our mind directly through the appropriate avenues of sense. That is to say, they no longer appeal primarily to the senses, but to the imagination.

And this appeal to the imagination is the characteristic quality of every form of poetry, whether its intention be pathetic or humorous, whether it present a picture of human life or of nature. In other words, whereas Aristotle found the key to one form of poetry only, Addison found a key that would unlock not only tragedy, but every other form of poetry as well.

But we must consider the nature of this appeal to the imagination a little more closely.

Up to the present the description of the poet and the picture of the painter have, broadly speaking, been treated by Addison (following in the steps of Aristotle) as appealing to the mind in precisely the same way as the originals on which these representations are respectively based appeal to the mind.[1] Aristotle, in distinguishing the truth

[1] Perhaps we should make an exception of the 'disagreeable objects' which Aristotle noticed could be represented by art without affecting the mind in the same way as the objects themselves did.

of art from the truth of logic, discovered a difference between the productions of art and the external realities on which these representations are based. Addison, using the fresh knowledge of his age, further discovers a difference between the manner in which natural objects and works of art respectively approach the mind. The picture, the statue, the written or spoken words, the *mise en scène*, do, indeed, approach the mind through the avenue of the senses, but these representations possess something more than the originals ; and the possession of this something causes them to use the avenue of the senses in a different manner. In other words, they are themselves in part the product of the imagination, and they, therefore, excite the imagination more keenly than the originals. This 'something,' then, which gives them their distinctive character and value as works of art, is the fact that they themselves embody the working of the imagination of the artist ; since by virtue of this embodiment, they appeal with especial force to the imagination of the mind which receives the sense-impressions produced by their sensible attributes. So Addison did for criticism what Descartes did for philosophy. He applied the idealistic principle in a form suited to the inquiry in question.

Stated in philosophic form the principle is this. In poetry and the fine arts, as in knowledge, there is something more than can be accounted for by the action of the senses. The painter, or the poet, produces in his work something more than he received by eye or ear, or by any combination of sense perceptions. The additional matter is due to a special process of the human mind, and the working of this process can for convenience be distinguished from the working of the mind in general as the 'faculty' of the imagination.

But Addison does not fall into the error of supposing that this selection of one aspect of the synthetic action of the mind is anything more than a device to facilitate the treatment of the subject. 'We divide the soul,' he says,[1] 'into several powers and faculties,' but 'there is no such Division in the Soul itself, since it is the whole Soul that remembers, understands, wills, or imagines. Our manner of considering the Memory, Understanding, Will, Imagination, and the like Faculties, is for the better enabling us to express ourselves in such Abstracted Subjects of Speculation, not that there is any such Division in the soul itself.' Addison's work is a case in point. For the treatment of the imagination as a separate faculty of the mind, led him to discover a new principle in criticism.

The manner in which he arrived at this new principle of criticism is worthy of notice. In all departments of his literary researches the growth of his thought is remarkable. *Solvitur ambulando* is a motto which is applicable throughout. In the present case he commences with an examination of the *effects* of the imagination writ large in man's intercourse with material existences. The group of papers, in which the principle is revealed, he terms 'this Essay on the Pleasures of the Imagination.' From a consideration of the general effects of the imagination he is led to observe, that in the satisfaction derived from poetry and the arts, the element of that satisfaction which is directly traceable to this faculty is predominant. And from this discovery he almost unconsciously adopts the opinion that the most successful efforts of poetry and

[1] *Spectator*, 600.

the arts are those in which the element of imagination is most developed. From this point he again advances to the position that art, if it is to be successful, must be capable of affecting the imagination ; that, in short, art and the artist should deliberately aim at this object. And if this be so, it follows that the test which criticism will chiefly apply is not any formal test of obedience to rules of construction, but the higher and spiritual test of ability to speak to the mind through this faculty of the imagination, however this grand object of artistic effort may be accomplished.

To illustrate this course of reasoning, we will approach the text of the Essay.

After remarking that 'our Sight is the most perfect and most delightful of all our senses,' he proceeds : [1]

'It is this Sense which furnishes the Imagination with its Ideas ; so that by the Pleasures of the Imagination or Fancy (which I shall use promiscuously) I here mean such as arise from visible Objects, either when we have them actually in our View, or when we call up their Ideas in our Minds by Paintings, Statues, Descriptions, or any the like Occasion. We cannot indeed have a single Image in the Fancy that did not make its first entrance through the Sight ; but we have the power of retaining, altering, and compounding those Images, which we have once received, into all the Varieties of Picture and Vision that are most agreeable to the Imagination ; for by this Faculty a Man in a Dungeon is capable of entertaining himself with Scenes and Landskips more beautiful than any that can be found in the whole Compass of Nature.'

By the pleasures of the imagination, he continues, are meant 'only such pleasures as arise originally

[1] Ib., 411.

from sight.' And these pleasures are divided into two kinds :

' My Design being first of all to discourse of those Primary Pleasures of the Imagination which proceed from such Objects as are before our Eyes ; and in the next place to speak of those Secondary Pleasures of the Imagination which flow from the Ideas of visible Objects, when the objects are not actually before the Eye, but are called up into our Memories, or formed into agreeable Visions of Things that are either Absent or Fictitious.'

Further, these pleasures are ' not so gross as those of Sense, nor so refined as those of the Understanding.' And they are useful, therefore, as a means of recreation.

They ' do not require such a Bent of Thought as is necessary to our more serious Employments, nor, at the same time, suffer the Mind to sink into that Negligence and Remissness, which are apt to accompany our more sensual Delights, but, like a gentle Exercise to the Faculties, awaken them from Sloth and Idleness, without putting them upon any Labour or Difficulty.'

The primary pleasures proceed from the sight of outward objects ; but what is it in those outward objects which especially appeals to the imagination ? According to Addison, the Great, the Uncommon or Strange, and the Beautiful. Moreover, he notices that the satisfaction thus derived through the sense of sight is increased by the presence of other qualities, revealed by other senses, in the same objects.

' Thus if there arises a Fragrancy of Smells or Perfumes, they heighten the pleasures of the Imagination, and make even the Colours and Verdure of the Landskip appear more agreeable ;

for the Ideas of both Senses recommend each other, and are pleasanter together than when they enter the Mind separately : As the different Colours of a Picture, when they are well disposed, set off one another, and receive an additional Beauty from the Advantage of their Situation.' [1]

As a means of contributing to the *primary* pleasures of the imagination, Addison decides that the works of art are inferior to those of nature. The art which is most successful in producing these primary pleasures is Architecture ; for the elements which chiefly constitute its beauty are bulk and proportion, and of these both are perceived directly by the sense of sight.

Addison now proceeds to consider the secondary pleasures of the imagination. These are caused, not by the sight of any natural objects, but by the ' calling up ' of such objects ' into the mind, either barely by its own operations, or on occasion of something without us, as Statues, or Descriptions.' [2]

The secondary pleasures, then, are due in all cases to representations of real objects. But these representations are of two kinds. In the first, the representation is itself a material reality perceptible by the sense of sight—the sense to which the imagination owes its existence—a cathedral, a picture, a *mise en scène*. In the second, there is no material reality perceptible to the sight, as in the case of a musical composition or a poem. In all these instances, he tells us, the secondary pleasures of the imagination proceed ' from that action of the mind, which compares the ideas arising from the original objects with the ideas we receive from the Statue, Picture, Description, or Sound that represents them.'

1 Ib., 412.   2 Ib., 416.

He then addresses himself especially to that class of these pleasures which arises from ideas 'raised by words'; that is to say, he confines himself to a consideration of the medium of literature. But in so doing he distinctly affirms that the principle of the poetic appeal to the mind is the principle of the appeal of the arts in general. 'Most of the observations,' he says, 'that agree with descriptions are equally applicable to Painting and Statuary.'

There are two methods in which the power of the imagination is manifested in relation to poetry. By the first it operates in the poet's mind; by the second, it operates in the mind of the hearer or reader. The appeal to the imagination which is addressed by poetry (and the arts) produces the second of these two operations. In the first operation the imagination is represented as producing (generally, and not in the poet or artist alone) what Addison calls its 'primary pleasures.' These 'primary pleasures' are produced by the action of the imagination in the mind of a man when his senses are under the influence of external stimuli. Where, however, these external stimuli take the form of works of art, such as pictures or statues, to these 'primary' pleasures are added 'secondary' pleasures, which arise, in the main, from a comparison of the artistic representation with the remembrance of the original object retained in the mind of the spectator. When, again, words are the only medium employed, and the 'representation' becomes a 'description,' the pleasures produced are entirely secondary; and, therefore, it is only these secondary pleasures of the imagination that poetry can command.[1]

[1] See p. 16.

Of the first operation—the action of the imagination in the mind of the poet—Addison writes :

‘ A Poet should take as much pains in forming his Imagination as a Philosopher in cultivating his Understanding. He must gain a due Relish of the works of Nature, and be thoroughly conversant in the various Scenary of a Country Life.

‘ When he is stored with Country Images, if he would go beyond pastoral, and the lower kinds of Poetry, he ought to acquaint himself with the Pomp and Magnificence of Courts. He should be very well versed in everything that is noble and stately in the Productions of Art, whether it appear in Painting or Statuary, in the great Works of Architecture which are in their present Glory, or in the Ruins of those which flourished in former Ages.

‘ Such advantages as these help to open a Man’s thoughts, and to enlarge his Imagination, and will therefore have their Influence upon all kinds of Writing, if the author knows how to make right use of them.’ [1]

And the use to which the imagination thus developed is to be put, is thus described :

‘ Because the Mind of Man requires something more perfect in Matter, than what it finds there, and can never meet with any sight in Nature which sufficiently answers its highest ideas of Pleasantness ; or, in other words, because the Imagination can fancy to itself Things more Great, Strange, or Beautiful, than the Eye ever saw, and is still sensible of some defect in what it has seen ; on this account it is the part of a Poet to humour the Imagination in its own Notions, by mending and perfecting Nature where he describes a Reality ; and by adding greater Beauties than are put together in Nature, where he describes a Fiction.

‘ He is not obliged to attend her in the slow Advances which

[1] *Spectator,* 417.

she makes from one Season to another, or to observe her Conduct
in the successive Production of Plants and Flowers. He may
draw into his Description all the Beauties of the Spring and
Autumn, and make the whole Year contribute to render it the
more agreeable. His Rose-trees, Woodbines, and Jessamines
may flower together, and his Beds be cover'd at the same time
with Lilies, Violets, and Amaranths. His Soil is not restrained
to any particular Sett of Plants, but is proper either for Oaks or
Mirtles, and adapts itself to the Products of every Climate.
Oranges may grow wild in it; Myrrh may be met with in every
Hedge, and if he thinks it proper to have a Grove of Spices, he
can quickly command Sun enough to raise it. If all this will
not furnish out an agreeable Scene, he can make several new
Species of Flowers, with richer Scents and higher Colours than
any that grow in the Gardens of Nature. His Consorts of
Birds may be as full and harmonious, and his Woods as thick
and gloomy as he pleases. He is at no more Expence in a
long Vista, than a short one, and can as easily throw his Cascades
from a Precipice half a Mile high, as from one of Twenty
Yards. He has his Choice of the Winds, and can turn the
Course of his Rivers in all the Variety of Meanders, that are
most delightful to the Reader's Imagination. In a word, he
has the modelling of Nature in his own Hands, and may give
her what Charms he pleases, provided he does not reform
her too much, and run into Absurdities, by endeavouring to
excel.' [1]

Of the second operation—the action of the imagination
of the hearer or reader whose mind is stimulated by the
words of the poet—he says :

' Words, when well chosen, have so great a Force in them,
that a Description often gives us more lively Ideas than the
Sight of Things themselves. The Reader finds a Scene drawn

[1] Ib., 418.

in stronger Colours, and painted more to the Life in his Imagination, by the help of Words, than by an actual Survey of the Scene which they describe. In this case the Poet seems to get the better of Nature; he takes, indeed, the Landskip after her, but gives it more vigorous Touches, heightens its Beauty, and so enlivens the whole Piece that the Images which flow from the Objects themselves appear weak and faint, in Comparison of those that come from the Expressions. The Reason, probably, may be because in the Survey of any Object we have only so much of it painted on the Imagination, as comes in at the Eye; but in its Description the poet gives us as free a View of it as he pleases, and discovers to us several parts, that either we did not attend to, or that lay out of our Sight when we first beheld it. As we look on any Object, our Idea of it is, perhaps, made up of two or three simple Ideas; but when the Poet represents it, he may either give us a more complex Idea of it, or only raise in us such Ideas as are most apt to affect the Imagination.' [1]

It will be observed that here Addison again avails himself of the results of Descartes' work in philosophy. He makes use of the Cartesian theory of association of ideas, to provide a psychological basis for the spiritual element which he has introduced into his account of the process of art. He afterwards dwells more at length on this theory, and uses it in particular to explain the fact that the pleasurable aspects of events or of objects which have been impressed upon the mind through the senses are uppermost in the picture which they leave behind in the mind. The 'sett of ideas,' he says, arising from a prospect have a 'sett of traces' belonging to them in the brain.

'But because the Pleasure we received from these Places far surmounted, and overcame the little Disagreeableness we

1 Ib., 416.

found in them; for this Reason there was at first a wider passage worn in the Pleasure Traces, and, on the contrary, so narrow a one in those which belonged to the disagreeable ideas, that they were quickly stopped up, and rendered incapable of receiving any Animal Spirits, and consequently of exciting any unpleasant ideas in the Memory.' [1]

And this explanation is applied generally to all cases in which the mind acts as a sort of filter, when for example, scenes of horror, or repulsive objects, as presented through the description of the poet, produce an agreeable instead of a disagreeable effect.

He sums up by the direct application of his psychological researches to literature, and it is this application which introduced a new principle into criticism.

' It is this Talent of affecting the Imagination that gives an Embellishment to Good Sense, and makes one Man's Compositions more agreeable than another's. It sets off all Writings in general, but is the very Life and highest Perfection of Poetry: Where it shines in an eminent degree, it has preserved several Poems for many Ages, that have nothing else to recommend them; and where all the other Beauties are present, the Work appears dry and insipid, if this single one be wanting. It has something in it like Creation; it bestows a kind of Existence, and draws up to the Reader's View several Objects which are not to be found in Being. It makes Additions to Nature, and gives a greater Variety to God's works. In a word, it is able to beautifie and adorn the most illustrious Scenes in the Universe, or to fill the Mind with more glorious Shows and Apparitions than can be found in any Part of it.' [2]

[1] Ib., 417.   [2] Ib., 421.

CHAPTER VI

BY the work of Addison criticism was brought into line
with modern thought ; and the critic was provided with
a test which he could apply with equal success to every
fresh form which literature had developed. Henceforth
it was recognised that the primary appeal of poetry was
addressed not to the understanding, nor to the senses, but
to the imagination. It was soon admitted that the same
thing was true, though in lesser degrees, of the Fine
Arts. All that was required for the extension of the
principle was to add definiteness to Addison's conception : to note the distinctions which marked the various
methods severally employed by the arts, and the consequent limits within which the principle could in each
case be applied ; and to define and explain the character
of the service performed by the imagination in the mind
of the artist.

In order to do this a return was necessarily made
to the methods of artistic (or formal) criticism. In
Germany, Lessing wrote his *Laocoon*, which was
published in 1766, and showed how the method of
Painting, as typical of the plastic and graphic arts,
differed from the method of Poetry, as representative of
music and creative literature, ' in which the method of

imitation is progressive.' And in thus distinguishing
between the method of Painting and that of Poetry, he
recognises the appeal to the imagination as that by which
the respective limits of the two typical arts are determined. For in order to know what this distinction is,
it is necessary first to ascertain to what extent, and in
what degree, each can rely upon the senses and the
imagination respectively for its effects.

It is necessary to make this point clear at the outset
of our consideration of Lessing's work, because, although
it is nowhere definitely stated, as far as I know, in the
Laocoon, it is nevertheless evident that his criticism
is coloured throughout by the new principle of poetic
appeal which was established by Addison. The sequel
will, I think, make this plain ; but in the meanwhile I
draw the attention of the reader to two passages which
directly illustrate the contention advanced.

The first of these passages occurs in the course of
Lessing's comparison of Virgil's description of the death
of Laocoon, with the sculptured representation of the
same subject which gives the title to his treatise. He
writes :

'Admitted that every detail which the word-painting poet
uses cannot have an equally good effect on the plain surface
of the painter's canvas, or in the sculptor's marble, is it not
possible, on the other hand, that each detail of which the
artist avails himself may be used with equal effect in the
work of the poet ? Undoubtedly ; for the beauty of a work
of art is revealed to us not by our eye, but by our imagination through the eye. A given image may be aroused in
our imagination, either by the symbols we ourselves choose to
use for that purpose or by natural symbols, and in each case

it must be accompanied by an identical feeling of pleasure, although the intensity of this pleasure may vary.' [1]

Here he states the principle that the ultimate appeal of all art is to the imagination through the senses. And in the following passage he tells us why the poet is restricted in the use of these symbols 'which we ourselves choose,' and in so doing he indicates to how much greater an extent the appeal of poetry is directed to the imagination than is the appeal of painting.

'The case is as follows. Since the symbols of speech are symbols adopted by ourselves, it is perfectly possible for us by means of them to indicate the consecutive appearance of the parts of a body as completely as we can perceive those same parts of a body in juxtaposition in nature. But this is an attribute of speech and of its symbols in general, an attribute, too, which does not minister specially to the purposes of poetry. The poet's object is not merely to be intelligible ; his representations must be something more than clear and distinct (*this* is sufficient for the prose writer). He desires to make the ideas which he arouses in us so vivid that, as they flash through our mind, we believe that we are experiencing the true, objective impressions produced by the physical originals of those ideas, and in this moment of our illusion we cease to be conscious of the medium which he employs for this purpose, that is, his words. It is this principle which forms the basis of the explanation of the poetical picture.' [2]

It is this principle, then, of the appeal to the imagination which forms the distinction between the respective methods of Painting and Poetry ; but Lessing establishes the distinction not by reference to this principle, but by

[1] *Laocoon*, vi. Blümner's text (Berlin, 1876).
[2] xvii.

defining the limits within which the painter and the poet
can respectively produce successful representations of the
real. And in adopting this point of view—that is to say,
by considering primarily the limits of these typical arts as
illustrated in the works of painter and poet, and not the
psychological principle to which these limits are due—he
returns, as I have already said, to the methods of formal
criticism.

The *Laocoon* commences with a discussion of the interesting question of the period at which the famous
sculptured group, so named, was produced. Although
he neglects no available evidence afforded by antiquarian
research, or by the direct testimony of classical authors,
he suggests that the question may be decided on artistic
grounds. For this purpose he compares Virgil's description with the work of the artist.[1] In both, Laocoon and
his two sons are represented as locked together in the
fatal embrace of the two serpents. This accord between
Virgil's description and the sculptured representation of
the scene is the more remarkable, since the idea which is
embodied is at variance with the common Greek account,
which relates that the children only, and not the father,

[1] I use the singular for the sake of clearness. Lessing (as, of course,
is the fact) attributes the Laocoon to Agesander, Polydorus, and
Athenodorus ; but his inference that they flourished in the period of
the early Cæsars, executing the work in question for some imperial
patron, perhaps at the suggestion of Pollio, is not established. The
Laocoon statue was found near the baths of Titus in 1506. It is
identified as the work of which Pliny wrote (*Nat. Hist.* xxxvi. c. 5)
as being in the palace of Titus, and as the work of three Rhodian
sculptors (Agesander, &c.). He says that it was produced *de consilii
sententia.* If this be rendered 'according to a commission *ad hoc,*' it
points to the time of Titus as the date of the Laocoon group. But if
it be taken to mean ' by a design formed in consultation,' it points to
a period shortly posterior to the death of Alexander.

were destroyed by the serpents. The strange similarity
makes it highly probable that either the poet imitated
the artist, or the artist imitated the poet. Now this
latter point, Lessing argues, can be decided by an examination of the details of the two representations; and
this examination will afford a useful object-lesson in the
subject of his study—the limits of painting and poetry.
If, in the course of this examination, we find that the
variations, which Virgil's description shows in comparison
with the sculpture, are such as can be attributed to the
limitations of poetry, we may conclude that the poet
copied the artist; if, on the other hand, we find that
the variations which the sculpture shows in comparison
with the description, are such as can be attributed to the
limitations of painting (as representing the plastic arts),
then we shall conclude that the artist copied the poet.

It is probable that neither of these alternatives represents
the fact. This, however, does not affect the value of
Lessing's inquiries, and before he supports this opinion, as
he does ultimately, by antiquarian evidence, he adopts it
as a hypothesis upon which he can build the structure of
his argument.

Assuming, then, that the artist imitated the poet,
Lessing finds that the sculptured representation of the
scene differs from the description given by Virgil in
certain important respects; but he shows that all of these
variations can be properly referred to the limitations of
the art of sculpture.

In the first place, Virgil describes Laocoon as uttering
appalling shrieks; but the countenances of the Laocoon
group are marked by the calmness and restraint characteristic of Greek art. Here we have a variation, but one

which can be directly referred to the requirements of the art employed. The sculptor 'must soften shrieks into sighs : not because a shriek reveals an ignoble soul, but because it causes the countenance to assume a repulsive form. For, only imagine the mouth of the Laocoon to be forced open, and judge of the effect. We let him shriek, and look. What is the result ? A form which before commanded compassion by displaying a union of beauty and pain, has now been changed into one that is merely ugly and repulsive, one from which we gladly turn our eyes away, because the look of pain arouses displeasure, while there is no beauty in the suffering object to convert this displeasure into the sweet feeling of compassion.' [1]

Again, the sculptor has departed from Virgil's disposition of the coils of the serpents.

> ' Bis medium amplexi, bis collo squamea circum
>   Terga dati, superant capite et cervicibus altis.'

That is to say, the serpents wind their coils twice round Laocoon's middle, and twice round his neck.

'This picture fills our imagination admirably : the noblest parts are compressed to suffocation, and the poison goes straight towards the face. But for all this it was not a picture for the artist—a picture, that is, which would exhibit the effect of the poison and of the pain in the body. For in order to display this it was necessary that the principal parts should be as free as possible, and that no external pressure should be anywhere applied to them which could change and weaken the play of the suffering nerves and working muscles. The double coils of the serpents would have hidden the whole body, and that grievous contraction

[1] II.

of the abdomen, which is so expressive, would have been unseen. What remained visible of the body, over, or under, or between the coils, would have appeared in a condition of contraction or distension, which would not have expressed the internal pain but the external pressure. The double coils similarly assigned by Virgil to the neck would have entirely destroyed the effect of the pyramidal acumination which makes the group so pleasant to the eye; and the pointed heads of the serpents thus extended from the mass into the air would have formed such a violent departure from proportion, that the composition of the figures as a whole would have become to the highest degree repellent. . . . The ancient sculptors realized at a glance the fact that their art made an entire change necessary. They transferred all the coils from the body and neck to the thighs and feet. Here these coils could conceal and compress as much as was required without affecting the expression injuriously; here, moreover, they produced the idea of checked flight and of a sort of immobility, which is so effective in aiding an artistic representation of a prolonged scene to acquire an appearance of continuity.' [1]

Once more, there is the absence of drapery. Virgil's Laocoon wears his priestly garments, but the figures in the sculptured group are entirely nude. Here, again, is a variation obviously to be referred to a difference in the medium of representation.

' A garment is no garment for the poet; it hides nothing; our imagination sees beneath it everywhere. It is all one to Virgil whether Laocoon has or has not his garment, for his pain is at all times and in every part of his body equally visible to the imagination. So far as the imagination goes, his forehead can be bound with the priestly chaplet without being hidden. Indeed, this chaplet, instead of detracting

[1] V.

from the conception which we form of the misfortune of the sufferer, strengthens it :

"Perfusus sanie vittas atroque veneno."

His priestly dignity is unavailing; even the symbols which universally command respect and reverence for his person are stained and desecrated with the poisonous spume.'

But the artist, on the other hand, had to present the agony of Laocoon's mind to the eye; and this he could do best, if not solely, by exhibiting the contortion and distortion of his body and limbs.

'By merely leaving Laocoon his chaplet, he would have signally weakened the expression. The forehead would have been in part hidden, and the forehead is the seat of expression. Just as in the former case he refrained from representing the shriek because it was inconsistent with beauty; so now he abandons the conventional chaplet in order to gain expression.' [1]

Having shown that his opinion that the artist copied the poet is supported thus far by artistic considerations, he proceeds to still further strengthen it by an examination of the weakness of the alternative proposition. 'I will now,' he says, 'take the opposite supposition : the poet shall have imitated the artist.'

First,[2] we must account for Virgil's introduction of the appalling shrieks. Now there is nothing unpoetic in this aspect of Virgil's description, but it is inconsistent with the assumption that he based his conception of the scene upon the Laocoon group.

'The artist,' says Lessing, 'had the most urgent reasons for not allowing the pain of Laocoon to find expression in shrieks.

[1] V.

[2] I do not follow the order of Lessing's successive arguments.

But if the poet had had before him the affecting union of pain and beauty afforded by the work of art, what consideration was there sufficiently weighty to account for his total omission of any attempt to render the conception of manly dignity and high-souled patience which arises out of this union of pain and beauty, and for his suddenly alarming us with the hideous outcry of Laocoon ? ' [1]

> ' Clamores simul horrendos ad sidera tollit :
> Quales mugitus, fugit cum saucius aram
> Taurus, et incertam excussit cervice securim.' [2]

In the second place, if Virgil had been inspired by the sight of the sculptured group of figures, he would have indicated more clearly in his description that which is the chief merit of the sculptor's work—the entanglement of the three figures in a knot of serpents' coils. His words are :

> ' illi agmine certo
> Laocoonta petunt : et primum parva duorum
> Corpora natorum serpens amplexus uterque
> Implicat, et miseros morsu depascitur artus.
> Post, ipsum auxilio subeuntem ac tela ferentem
> Corripiunt, spirisque ligant ingentibus : et jam
> Bis medium amplexi, bis collo squamea circum
> Terga dati, superant capite et cervicibus altis.' [3]

Thus, says Lessing, he is content ' to subdue the expression of the entanglement of all three bodies in a single knot to an extent which leaves it to conjecture.' But if he had seen the entanglement as the sculptor presented it :

' It would have appealed to his eye so vividly; the effect which it would have produced upon him would have been so

[1] VI.   [2] *Æneid*, ii. l. 222–4.   [3] Ib., 212–219.

powerful, as to compel him to give it greater prominence in his description. As I have already said, this was not the time to describe the entanglement in detail. Quite true; but a single word more would have given it a decided emphasis in the subordinate position in which the poet was bound to keep it. What the artist could reveal without this word, the poet would not have grudged a word to express, had he seen it rendered by the artist.' [1]

Nor would Virgil the poet have altered the coils of the serpents. 'These find employment for the hands and bind the feet in the work of art. This disposal of them secures pleasure for the eye, and a vivid picture for the imagination, in equal degrees.'

And so, after again remarking that the material alteration in the traditional account of the scene must be held to have been made by Virgil, he writes in conclusion :

" It follows that if, in view of this entanglement which both adopt, there is to be imitation on one side or the other, it is more reasonable to suppose that it is on the side of the artist rather than on that of the poet. In all else the one deviates from the other. But there is this distinction to be observed. When the artist has made the deviations, these deviations are not inconsistent with the supposition that he intended to imitate the poet ; since the scope and limits of his art make them necessary for him. If, on the other hand, we assume that it is the poet who has been the imitator, then all the deviations to which I have alluded go to disprove the assumed imitation, and those persons who support this theory in the face of such evidence can have no other object in view than to assert that the work of art is older than the poet's description.' [2]

In the course of this discussion of the Laocoon, Lessing had already decided that his hypothesis, that the artist

[1] VI. [2] Ib.

imitated the poet, did not in any degree lessen the merit
of his work. He subsequently returns to the question
thus incidentally raised, and decides the general question
of the relative merit of invention in the Painter and Poet
by reference to the nature of their respective arts.
'How is it,' he asks, 'that we do not in any degree lessen
our admiration for the artist, when all that he has done
is to represent the words of the poet through the medium
of form and colour?' The answer is that, 'in the case
of the artist, execution appears to us to be more difficult
than invention, while in the case of the poet the position
is reversed, and execution appears to us to be easier than
invention.' [1] And he embodies his argument in two
propositions : 'Firstly, invention and novelty of subject
is not by any means the most important quality of the
painter ; and, secondly, familiarity of subject assists and
facilitates the operation of his art.' [2]

From this position he proceeds by a natural transition
to consider the nature of this 'execution' which is the
all-important element in the artist's work. For this
purpose he analyses certain scenes from Homer in conjunction with those which Count Caylus has selected [3]
from the same poet as affording subjects for paintings.
Why is it, he asks, that some scenes are selected, and
others rejected? Because a 'poetic' picture is not
the same thing as an 'artistic' picture. In the first
place, 'the artist must necessarily renounce whole
classes of pictures which the poet has always at his
disposal.' Homer represents invisible actions and persons

[1] XI.   [2] Ib.

[3] In *Tableaux tirés de l'Iliade, de l'Odysée d'Homère et de l'Enéide de Virgile,
avec des Observations générales sur le costume :* à Paris, 1757–8.

as well as visible; Dryden's 'Ode upon St. Cecilia's Day' is full of 'musical pictures' which cannot be reproduced by the methods of painting. And, therefore, he decides incidentally that Count Caylus's theory, that 'suitability to the painter' is the test of poetic merit, that poets must be ranked 'according to the number of paintings which they afford the artist,' breaks down. On the contrary, says Lessing :

'A poetical picture is not necessarily one which can be converted into a material picture. But every detail, every combination of several details, which enables the poet to make his description of an object so distinct that we are more conscious of this object than of his words, is said to be picturesque, is said to be a picture, because it makes us approach that degree of illusion which the material picture is especially capable of producing, and of which the material picture is the primary and most ready source.' [1]

And in the second place, even in the case of visible objects which both arts can alike represent, the 'poetical picture' does not always provide the painter with a subject; nor, on the other hand, does a painting always afford the poet a scene which he can effectively reproduce. Why is it that poetical pictures of visible objects are useless for the painter? Lessing answers this question by exhibiting two Homeric pictures in contrast.

'The picture of Pandarus,' he says, 'is one of the most highly finished and effective in the whole of Homer. From the seizing of the bow to the flight of the arrow, every moment is painted, and all the moments which are selected are so clearly marked, in spite of the closeness with which they follow each other, that if we did not know how to set about using a bow we

[1] XIV.

could learn to do so merely from this word-picture. Pandarus draws his bow forward, fixes the string on it, opens the quiver, chooses a well-feathered arrow which has never been used, places the arrow on the string, draws the string back together with the arrow below at the notch, draws the string close up to his breast, and the iron arrow-head to the bow, the great bent bow flies apart with a clang, the string vibrates, the arrow is sped and flies swiftly towards its goal.' [1]

Αὐτὰρ ὁ σύλα πῶμα φαρέτρης, ἐκ δ' ἕλετ' ἰὸν
ἀβλῆτα πτερόεντα, μελαινέων ἕρμ' ὀδυνάων·
αἶψα δ' ἐπὶ νευρῇ κατεκόσμει πικρὸν ὀϊστὸν

.   .   .   .

ἕλκε δ' ὁμοῦ γλυφίδας τε λαβὼν και νεῦρα βόεια·
νευρὴν μὲν μαζῷ πελασεν, τόξῳ δε σίδηρον.
αὐτὰρ ἐπεὶ δὴ κυκλοτερὲς μέγα τόξον ἔτεινεν,
λίγξε βιὸς, νευρὴ δὲ μέγ' ἴαχεν, ἆλτο δ' ὀϊστὸς
ὀξυβελὴς, καθ' ὅμιλον ἐπιπτέσθαι μενεαίνων.[2]

Count Caylus, he says, cannot have overlooked this admirable picture. Why did he, therefore, consider it unsuitable for artistic treatment ? And why did he think that another scene, the gods assembled in council and drinking in the palace of Zeus—

Οἱ δὲ θεοὶ πὰρ Ζηνὶ καθήμενοι ἠγορόωντο
χρυσέῳ ἐν δαπέδῳ, μετὰ δὲ σφισι πότνια Ἥβη
νέκταρ ἐῳνοχόει· τοὶ δὲ χρυσέοις δεπάεσσιν
δειδέχατ' ἀλλήλους, Τρώων πόλιν εἰσορόωντες [3]—

was suitable for such treatment ?

The sharp contrast presented by these two scenes serves as a suitable introduction for a precise and detailed

---

[1] XV.   [2] *Iliad*, iv. 116–126.
[3] Ib., 1–4. Also p. 30 of *Tableaux*.

statement of the essential difference between the respective methods of these two typical arts.

Broadly put, Poetry represents what is in progression ; Painting, what is in juxtaposition. The reason why the first of these two scenes is unsuitable for representation by the painter lies in the fact that it embodies 'a visible and progressive action, the different parts of which happen one after another in sequence of time.' The reason why the second *is* suitable lies in the fact that it embodies 'a visible and stationary action, the different parts of which are developed in juxtaposition in space.' As a means of representing a landscape or a figure, Poetry is inferior to Painting ; as a means of representing action, and the working of the human mind in action, Poetry is superior to Painting. But Poetry can represent bodies by means of actions which reveal the characteristic properties of these bodies through progression. Painting, similarly, can represent action by means of bodies so disposed when stationary as to suggest progression. From these normal lines of effort, however, both arts depart ; and this departure, in which each continually leaves its respective sphere to trespass on that of the other, makes it exceedingly difficult, or rather impossible, to fix the exact limits within which each should respectively be confined.

When they meet on common ground in the representation of visible objects, they must select those aspects of such objects which are respectively appropriate to them. Poetry, says Lessing, 'employs articulate sounds *in time ;*' meaning thereby sounds which are successively uttered : and Painting 'forms and colours *in space,*' that is, which co-exist in juxtaposition.

'Objects which exist in juxtaposition, or objects the parts of which exist in juxtaposition, are called bodies. It follows, therefore, that bodies, with their visible attributes, are the special objects of painting.

'Objects which are successive, or objects the parts of which are successive, are called actions. It follows, therefore, that actions are the special objects of poetry.'

But painting can imitate action in a secondary degree.

'Yet all bodies exist not only in space, but also in time. They continue, and in each moment of their continuance they are able to assume a different appearance and to stand in a fresh relationship. Every one of these momentary appearances and relationships is the effect of a previous appearance or relationship, and can be the cause of a succeeding appearance or relationship, and consequently, as it were, the centre of an action. It follows, therefore, that painting can also imitate actions, but only by using bodies to suggest them.'

And poetry can similarly imitate bodies.

'On the other hand, actions cannot exist by themselves, but must exist in connection with certain beings. In so far as these beings are bodies, or are regarded as being bodies, poetry also represents bodies, but only by using actions to suggest them.'

Painting must therefore select one pregnant moment.

'In its co-existing compositions painting can use only one single moment of an action, and must therefore choose that moment which is most pregnant, and which indicates most clearly what has gone before and what is to follow.'

Poetry similarly must choose one property of bodies.

'It uses in its progressive imitations only a single property of bodies, and it must, therefore, select that property which awakens the most vivid picture of the body which it represents, as seen in that aspect which is most suitable for its purpose.' [1]

To take one of the simple examples by which Lessing illustrates his meaning, if the object to be represented be a ship, the painter reproduces upon his canvas so much of its form and colour as would meet the eye of the spectator at a single moment, and from a single point of view. But the poet adds to the appropriate word-symbol (ship) a single characteristic epithet—'the swift ship.' So, too, Homer paints a portrait—'Steadfast Penelope,' or 'Prudent Odysseus.' Nor is Homer alone in this.

'The art of the pen,' writes Mr. Meredith, ' is to rouse the inward vision, instead of labouring with a drop-scene brush, as if it were to the eye ; because our flying minds cannot contain a protracted description. That is why the poets, who spring imagination with a word or a phrase, paint lasting pictures. The Shakespearian, the Dantesque, are in a line, two at most.' [2]

Descriptions, then, whether of physical beauty or of nature, are *as such* outside the limits of the art of poetry. It is not that language is unable to represent 'a corporeal whole with its parts in due relationship ; ' it can do this because its symbols besides being consecutive can denote anything which we choose them to mean ; but, says Lessing, 'I refuse to allow this quality to language as the medium of poetry, because such verbal descriptions are entirely devoid of the illusion which constitutes so essential an element in poetry ; and I say that they must be devoid of this illusion, because the *co-existent* element in the body is inconsistent with the *consecutive* element of language.' [3] That is to say, if a description is to become

[1] XV. and XVI.   [2] *Diana of the Crossways*.   [3] XVII.

a poetical picture it must express extension in space by duration in time. In order to show how this can be done, Lessing turns again to Homer, and supports his contention by an examination of numerous passages. When Homer describes material objects, he does so by the proper method of poetry. He represents form by means of action. In the transcendent example of 'the shield of Achilles,' Lessing points out how Homer describes not the completed shield, but the several processes by which it was wrought and embellished, 'in a hundred magnificent lines;'[1] changing 'the co-existent in his subject into the consecutive, and thereby giving us a living picture of an action instead of a wearisome painting of a body.'

And especially is this true in respect of physical beauty.

'The poet, who can only depict the elements of beauty by describing them in order, entirely refrains, therefore, from the description of physical beauty as beauty. He feels that these elements, when presented consecutively, cannot possibly have the same effect as they would have if they were presented as parts of one whole; that the concentrating glance which we should at once throw back over them, would never present these elements to us in a single picture; that it is beyond the power of human imagination to picture the effect of a particular mouth, nose, and eyes, when combined in a countenance, unless we happen to be able to recall a countenance composed of similar elements from art or nature.'[2]

Once more Homer presents the 'example of examples.' When he wishes to convey to our minds a sense of the supreme beauty of Helen, he does not describe her

[1] *Iliad*, xviii. 483–508.   [2] XX.

form, but he tells us of the effect which the sight of her beauty produced upon the oldest and the wisest of the men of Troy.

Οὐ νέμεσις Τρῶας καὶ ἐϋκνήμιδας Ἀχαιοὺς
Τοιῇδ' ἀμφὶ γυναικὶ πολὺν χρόνον ἄλγεα πάσχειν·
αἰνῶς ἀθανάτῃσι θεῇς εἰς ὦπα ἔοικεν.[1]

The poet, therefore, is not deprived of the power of representing physical beauty by respecting the limits of his art. On the contrary, there is an aspect of physical beauty which, though it eludes the painter's grasp, is the special property of the poet. ' Charm,' says Lessing, ' is beauty in motion, and, for that very reason, is less suitable to the painter than to the poet. The painter can only suggest movement ; in reality his figures are motionless. It follows, therefore, that with him charm degenerates into caricature.' But in poetry it remains what it is : a ' transitory beauty which we wish to see again and again.' [2]

Finally, Lessing discusses the extent to which the poet and the painter can respectively avail themselves of physical ugliness. His criticism on this head forms a fitting complement of Addison's account of the ludicrous as an element of literature.[3]

Of the two the poet can avail himself far more freely of ugliness than the painter. That either can do so is due to the fact pointed out by Aristotle in the ' Poetics,' and traced to its psychological origin by Addison, that repulsive objects, as represented by art, are deodorised, as it were, by the action of the artist's mind. This purifying process is most effective in poetry ; and

[1] *Iliad*, iii. 156–8.   [2] XXI.   [3] Chapter iv. p. 77.

accordingly Lessing writes that the poet ' can use ugliness just because it becomes in his description a less repulsive appearance of bodily imperfection, and from the point of view of effect, ceases to be ugliness at all.' [1]

The poet, therefore, can make use of ugliness directly, but in addition to this primary use, he employs it as an ingredient to produce certain ' mixed feelings,' grouped under the respective heads of ' the ridiculous' and 'the horrible.'

Ugliness alone cannot produce the ridiculous : ' for ugliness is imperfection, and in order to create a sense of the ridiculous a contrast is required of perfections with imperfections.' Lessing then continues : ' This is the explanation of my friend, and I should like to add to it that this contrast must not be too sharply drawn, and that the *opposita*, to continue in the language of the painter, must be of such a sort that they can be blended into one another.' [2] The reference here is to the philosophic writings of Moses Mendelssohn ; [3] and it is scarcely necessary to point out the agreement of this passage with Addison's account of Wit,[4] in which we are told that the ' comparison of ideas' must be sufficiently veiled to afford the ' surprise' which forms one of its elements. In illustration of his meaning Lessing refers to Pope as an example of ugliness which was not ridiculous. ' The frail and deformed Pope,' he says, 'must have been much more interesting to his friends than the handsome and healthy Wycherley was to his.' And for an example of ugliness as the basis of the ridiculous he refers once again to Homer. ' Thersites does not become ridiculous by

[1] XXIII.   [2] Ib.
[3] Vol. ii. p. 23.   [4] See chapter iv. p. 79.

mere ugliness; at the same time he would not be ridiculous if he were not ugly. The ugliness, the agreement of this ugliness with his character, the contrast which both of these present with the idea which he cherishes of his own importance, the effect of his spiteful talkativeness—harmless to others, hurtful only to himself—all alike unite in producing this sense of the ridiculous.' [1]

The horrible is ugliness when painful. In order to produce a sense of the ridiculous, the contrast afforded by the ugly with the superior person (or object) must not appeal to our sympathies or even our emotions; in that case it becomes (as Aristotle says) not comic, but tragic. Lessing still goes to the same character, Thersites, for his illustration, but Quintus Calaber and not Homer is the poet.[2]

'Achilles is grieved because he has killed Penthesilea. As she lies in her blood, shed so bravely, her beauty compels the respect and the compassion of the hero; and respect and compassion become love. But in the mind of the slanderous Thersites this love of his assumes the complexion of a crime. He harangues against the lust which leads even the noblest of men into folly.

> . . . ἥτ᾽ ἄφρονα φῶτα τίθησι
> καὶ πινυτόν περ ἐόντα.

Achilles is enraged, and without a word in reply, deals him a blow so terrible between the cheek and ear that teeth and blood and life all come forth together from his mouth. It is horrible. The passionate, murderous Achilles becomes more hateful to me than the knavish, snarling Thersites. The cry of exultation which the Greeks raise over this deed offends

---

[1] XXIII. [2] *Paralipomena*, i. 720-778.

me. I range myself on the side of Diomedes, who is already drawing his sword to exact vengeance for his kinsman on the murderer : at this moment I am conscious that Thersites is also my kinsman, since he is a man.' [1]

The painter, owing to the character of the medium which he employs, is more restricted in the use of ugliness. 'Painting,' says Lessing, 'as a method of imitation can express ugliness ; painting as a fine art declines to do so.' [2] For the aversion which arises from ugliness of form in real objects, arises also from the representation of these objects to the eye by form and colour. It is even doubtful, Lessing thinks, whether painting as a fine art is justified in using ugliness of form to produce the ridiculous and the horrible, although 'both of these by imitation attain a new degree of attractiveness and pleasurableness.' Here, in representing these mixed sensations, Painting is plainly at a disadvantage as compared with Poetry.

'In poetry,' says Lessing, 'as I have already remarked, ugliness of form loses its unpleasant effect almost entirely through the change of its co-existing parts into successive parts. It thereby ceases, as thus regarded, to be ugliness at all ; and, therefore, can unite itself so much the more intimately with other appearances as to produce a new and special effect. In painting, on the other hand, ugliness retains all its effects, and works scarcely less powerfully than it does when it is present in natural objects. Harmless ugliness cannot, therefore, long remain merely ludicrous. Our sense of what is unpleasant in it gains the upper hand, and what was at first comic grows to be simply detestable. The same result is found in the case of harmful ugliness ;

[1] XXIII.   [2] XXIV.

our sense of the horrible is gradually lost and deformity remains behind alone and unchangeable.' [1]

In this masterly way did Lessing warn the world of art against the danger of too hastily adopting Horace's generalisation—*ut pictura poesis.*

His work, like Aristotle's treatise, is, as he himself says, rather a series of rough notes for a book than a book itself. The deficiency of arrangement natural to a work so produced makes the *Laocoon* difficult reading ; and it is probably due to this circumstance that the mass of information which it contains is, comparatively speaking, even now unfamiliar. But what the *Laocoon* has lost in balance and literary finish it has gained in originality and force.

[1] XXIV.

CHAPTER VII

DEVELOPMENT OF PHILOSOPHIC (OR PLATONIC) CRITICISM BY COUSIN

HALF a century later Cousin followed Lessing with a 'regular and complete theory of Beauty and Art:' and it is significant that this complete account is not based upon the philosophy of Aristotle, but on that of Plato.

The contrast presented by a comparison of Cousin's work with that of Lessing is very instructive. Lessing begins with the study of a single work of art, Cousin with the principle of beauty. The method of Lessing is that of Aristotle, and like Aristotle he depends for the support of his conclusions upon examples taken from the existing works of artists and poets. Cousin is a disciple of Plato and Descartes: his method is idealistic—that is, philosophic in the one sense in which he admits the application of the term. The results which he obtains are less exact, less practical than those of Lessing, but they have a wider application and a more permanent validity.

The series of lectures entitled *Du Vrai, du Beau et du Bien*, were originally delivered in 1818; they were published from pupils' notes in 1836, and by the author himself in 1853. In the treatise which thus assumed its present literary form, Cousin ranges the results of a study, at once wide and exact, of ancient and modern philosophy under the three principles of the True, the Beautiful, and the Good. In thus making the study of the beautiful an integral part of philosophy, he claims that he is re-writing a chapter forgotten or omitted since the time of Plato and Aristotle.

Locke and Condillac, he says, have not left 'a single page upon beauty.' Diderot was, in the words of Voltaire, 'a head in which everything fermented without coming to maturity;' for he was ignorant of the principle of the ideal. Both the Scotch School, as represented by Hutcheson and Reid, and Kant found a place for the beautiful in their systems; but while they considered it as manifested in the soul and in nature, 'they did not even approach the difficult question of the reproduction of the beautiful by the genius of man.'

It is strange that Cousin should make no mention of the work of Addison or Lessing in this connection. It is scarcely credible, having in view the large space occupied by the imagination in Cousin's theory of art, and in particular certain passages which seem to be an adaptation of what Addison wrote on the power of the imagination, that he should have been ignorant of the nature of his work. On the other hand, Cousin's penetration was such that if he had studied the *Spectator* with any degree of attention, he must have recognised the essential difference between Addison and the crowd of pseudo-classical critics of the seventeeth century. The explanation seems to lie in the fact that Addison had already specialised that aspect of the subject which deals with the criticism of Literature. If this surmise be true—if, that, is to say, Cousin's failure to recognise Addison's work be due to the fact that he considers beauty as a part of philosophy—the circumstance supports the conclusion at which I have already arrived, that in Addison we have the first writer since Aristotle who was able to distinguish criticism from philosophy on the one hand, and from science on the other : the first genuine critic of literature, and the founder of literary criticism as such. The omission of Lessing must be referred similarly to the fact that he, though in a less degree, specialised criticism on its artistic side. In other words, Cousin fails to recognise the fact that criticism had already become a separate and distinct field of intellectual inquiry.[1]

For the rest, from his standpoint and within the limits of his design—'to offer at least an outline-sketch of a regular and complete theory of Beauty and Art'—Cousin's account is admirably conceived and executed. In the short space of four chapters he formulates and (within these limits) answers the four all-important questions upon the solution of which the certainty, and consequently the value, of criticism depends.

These questions are :—

I. What is subjective beauty, or what are the faculties to which we owe our idea of the beautiful ?

II. What is objective beauty, or what is it that makes a person, an action, a thought, or a thing beautiful ?

III. What is art, or how is the beautiful reproduced ?

IV. What separates the Fine Arts, or what are the means, and therefore the aims, which respectively belong to the several arts ?

Cousin at the very outset applies the central principle of his spiritual philosophy to distinguish the idea of beauty

[1] He refers incidentally to Lessing in Leçon ix., and to Addison in an earlier passage.

from any conception of the beautiful based upon the evidence of the senses.

If the idea of beauty has been conveyed to us by the senses it must be reducible into the agreeable ; for the senses cannot tell us that a thing is beautiful, but only that it is agreeable. But the idea of beauty cannot be so reduced. In the first place, experience shows that beauty and agreeableness are not interchangeable ; for it does not always follow that a thing which is agreeable is beautiful. In the second, of the five senses two only, hearing and sight, can arouse the idea of beauty. Indeed, ' sensation not only does not produce the idea of beauty, but it sometimes suffocates it.' [1]

Hence the fundamental distinction between the beautiful and the agreeable is the fact that beauty is discerned by ' reason ' and not by ' sensation.' In other words, the quality of beauty can be recognised by a judgment of universal validity ; and such a judgment cannot be pronounced by the senses, for their verdict is not absolute, but relative.

' Confound reason with sensibility, reduce the idea of beauty to the sensation of agreeableness, and taste has no longer any law. If a person tells me, in the presence of the Apollo Belvedere, that he does not find anything more agreeable in it than he does in any other statue, that this particular statue does not please him, and that he does not feel its beauty, I cannot dispute his impression ; but if this person concludes from this fact that the Apollo is not beautiful, I contradict him firmly, and I declare that he is mistaken. Correct taste is distinguished from incorrect taste, but this distinction is meaningless,

[1] P. 136. *Du Vrai, du Beau et du Bien,* par Victor Cousin. 27th edition. Paris: 1894.

if the recognition (*jugement*) of beauty is resolved into a sensation.'[1]

The test which gives validity to the recognition of beauty pronounced by reason, is the ideal : 'the idea of a higher beauty which Plato admirably calls the Form of beauty, and which, after him, all men of fine taste, all true artists, call the ideal. We establish degrees in the beauty of things because we compare them, often unconsciously, with this ideal which is the measure and the principle of all our judgments upon particular beauties. How,' he asks, 'could this idea of absolute beauty involved in all our judgments on the beautiful, how could this ideal beauty, which we cannot help conceiving, be revealed by sensation, by a faculty as variable and relative as the objects which it apprehends ? '[2]

The first faculty by which we perceive beauty is, therefore, reason.

The second faculty is sentiment or feeling. The idea of beauty cannot be referred to sentiment, although it is easier to refer it to sentiment than to sensation. If the idea of beauty depended upon the sentiment of beauty, and not upon reason and the test of the ideal, love of beauty would be indistinguishable from the desire for a beautiful object. But while desire aims at possession, the sentiment of beauty finds its satisfaction in itself. It is aroused, for example, by 'the discoveries of Descartes and Newton, by the exploits of the great Condé, and by the virtue of St. Vincent de Paul.' Sentiment, therefore, is not a principle, but 'a true and important fact'; and it 'plays a considerable part in the

[1] P. 138.   [2] Pp. 139 40.

perception of beauty.'[1] As the idea of beauty is a distinct (*simple*) idea, the sentiment of beauty is a special sentiment which manifests itself in two ways. There is the sentiment of beauty properly so called, which is based upon the perception of a harmony, and the sentiment of the sublime, which is based upon the perception of the infinite.

After reason and sentiment, the imagination is the next of the faculties which enter into the perception of beauty. On the one hand the imagination animates and vivifies reason and sentiment; on the other, it is itself stimulated by sentiment and controlled by taste. 'The gift of being strongly affected by objects and of reproducing the absent or vanished images of such objects, and the power of modifying these images and composing new images out of them,'[2] does not alone constitute the faculty of imagination. It must 'take its inspirations from sentiment, and become fruitful.'[3]

'It is therefore impossible,' he writes, 'to limit the imagination, as the word seems to require, to the images properly so called, and to the ideas which relate to physical objects. To recall sounds, to choose between them, to combine them so as to produce new effects from them, is not this also imagination, though a sound is not an image? The true musician does not possess less imagination than the poet. We grant the poet imagination when he brings back the images of nature; shall we refuse him this same faculty when he brings back sentiments or feelings? But, beside images and feelings, does not the poet employ the great thoughts of justice, liberty, virtue—in a word, all moral ideas? Shall we say that in these paintings of moral phenomena, in these pictures of the inner life of the soul, whether they delight or arouse us, there is no imagination?'[4]

[1] P. 140 onwards.   [2] P. 147.   [3] P. 148.   [4] Pp. 148–9.

Finally, there is the faculty of taste, which is not a separate faculty but 'a happy mingling' of reason, sentiment, and imagination.

For the appreciation of the works of the imagination it is necessary to have imagination in ourselves ; and therefore imagination is an essential constituent of correct taste. But there is one aspect of beauty, beauty of expression (*la beauté reglée*), to which the imagination is comparatively insensible. 'Unity in the composition, harmony of all the parts, the right proportion of accessory detail, the happy combination of effects, selection, balance, measure,'[1] are excellences which it can only slightly feel, and which it cannot properly appreciate. To estimate these at their true value it must be regulated and controlled by the taste which appreciates beauty, and which is identical with the genius which reproduces it.

According to Cousin, therefore, the faculties by which we perceive and appreciate beauty are reason, sentiment or feeling, imagination, and taste ; and by these faculties we are enabled to compare external beauty with the ideal beauty implanted in the soul by God. And, accordingly, subjective beauty is the conscious recognition of a greater or less similarity between external existences and the infinite perfection which we can only conceive of negatively—that is, as something neither human nor natural, but divine.

In order to reply to the second question—What is objective beauty ?—Cousin divides the subject into four heads : beauty in objects, the essence of beauty, its types and species, and its first and final principle.

[1] P. 152.

He has already shown that the equality which makes objects beautiful is not the 'agreeable'; he now further distinguishes it from the 'useful' and the 'suitable.' Neither can beauty be said to consist in proportion, order, or harmony, all of which can be resolved into 'unity.' But 'the theory which most approaches the facts is that which makes it consist of two contrary and equally necessary elements, unity and variety.'[1]

The joint manifestation of unity and variety is, therefore, the essence of beauty.

'Take a beautiful flower. Unity, order, proportion, even symmetry are unmistakably there; for without these qualities reason would be absent from it, and all things are made with a reason that passes understanding. But at the same time, what diversity! How many shades in the colour, what richness in the least details! Even in mathematics what is beautiful is not an abstract principle; it is this principle drawing with it a long chain of consequences. There is no beauty without life; and life, that is movement, is diversity.'[2]

The presence of these two elements, the essential characteristic of beauty, is to be found in all types and orders of beauty: in beauty properly so called, and in sublimity, in physical, intellectual, and moral beauty.

What gives unity to these three separate orders of beauty is the fact that they can be resolved into 'one and the same beauty, moral beauty, which includes in addition to moral beauty so called, all spiritual beauty.'[3] And moral beauty is, therefore, the foundation of physical beauty.

Cousin illustrates this conclusion by an examination of Winckelmann's analysis of the Apollo Belvedere.

[1] P. 158. [2] Ib. [3] P. 161.

'What arouses Winckelmann especially is the stamp of divinity imprinted in the immortal youth spread over the beautiful body, in the figure slightly taller than that of a man, in the majestic attitude, in the imperious movement, in the entire person and in all its details.   The brow is plainly that of a god ; an unalterable peace dwells there.   Lower down humanity reappears somewhat, and it is necessary—to interest man in the works of art.   In the satisfied glance, in the inflated nostrils, in the raising of the lower lip, anger mingled with disdain is seen, the pride of victory and the slight exertion which it has cost.   Weigh well every word of Winckelmann ; you will find it contains a moral impression.   The tone of the learned antiquary rises little by little to enthusiasm, and his analysis becomes a hymn of spiritual beauty.' [1]

So, too, the face of living man becomes beautiful when it is illuminated by the spirit within, and his figure is ennobled when it expresses the beauty of the soul. Even when man's figure is in repose, it has a higher beauty than that of an animal, because, 'even in the absence of virtue or genius, it always reflects an intelligent and moral nature.'   And the figure of an animal has a higher beauty than that of any inanimate object, because 'it reflects at least feeling, and something of the soul, if not the entire soul.'

If we chance upon a morsel of matter which expresses nothing, which means nothing, then and then only we have found something with which we cannot any longer associate the idea of beauty.   But 'all existence is animated, is ensouled.   Matter is changed and penetrated by forces which are not material, and it follows laws which give evidence of an ever-present intelligence.' [2]

[1] Pp. 162–3.   [2] P. 165.

And so 'the face of nature is as expressive as the face of man.'

'The form cannot be simply a form, it must be the form of something. Physical beauty is therefore the sign of an inner beauty which is spiritual and moral beauty, and here we have the foundation, the principle, the unity of beauty.' [1]

All these types of beauty are included in 'real' beauty. But, in addition to 'real' beauty, there is a beauty of a different order—'ideal' beauty.

'The ideal resides neither in a particular nor in a collection of particulars. Nature or experience provides us with the opportunity of conceiving it, but it is essentially different from them. For him who has once conceived it, all natural figures, however beautiful they may be, are only the images of a higher beauty which they cannot realise. Give me a noble action, I will imagine one which is still more noble. The very Apollo admits of more than one criticism. The ideal ever retires in proportion as it is more closely approached. Its last term is in the infinite, that is in God; or to speak more exactly the true and absolute ideal is none other than God Himself.' [2]

And, therefore, since the final manifestation of ideal beauty is God, God is the final principle of all beauty. He is the principle of the three orders of beauty, physical, intellectual, and moral beauty; and the two great forms of beauty, beauty and sublimity, which appear separately in these orders, are re-united in Him.

'Thus the absolute being, which is at one and the same time absolute unity and infinite variety, God, is necessarily the final cause, the ultimate basis, the realised (*accompli*) ideal of all beauty. Here we have that eternal beauty of which Diotima

[1] P. 166.　　　　　　　　　　[2] P. 166-7.

had caught a glimpse, and which she describes to Socrates in the *Symposium.*'

' " Oh, Socrates," ' continued the stranger from Mantinea, ' " what gives this life its value is the sight of the eternal beauty. . . . How unspeakably blessed would that mortal be to whom it should be given to contemplate absolute beauty, in its purity and simplicity, no longer clothed in flesh and human colour and in all those empty ornaments which are condemned to perish ; to whom it should be given to see face to face, under its proper (*unique*) form, the divine beauty." ' [1]

In the course of his reply to the third question—What is art? or how is beauty reproduced?—Cousin distinguishes certain principal elements which enter into the constitution of a work of art. But at the outset of his inquiry he places the imagination as the determining agency in its creation.

We want, he says, to see again, to feel again, the natural beauty, physical or moral, which delights us in the world of real life ; and we therefore attempt to reproduce it, *non pas telle qu'elle était, mais telle que notre imagination nous la représente. De là une œuvre originale et propre à l'homme, une œuvre d'art.*' [2]

Art, then, is the 'free reproduction of beauty,' and the faculty to which it is to be referred is 'genius.' Genius is a union of creative power with 'taste,' and this latter, as he has already explained, is itself a complex of imagination, feeling, and reason. Genius does not create in the sense of being 'the rival of God' ; nor does it merely 'imitate.' It finds its materials in Nature, but it reproduces them in a different form. This difference of form is due to the fact that the artist does not

[1] P. 170–1.   [2] P. 172

directly reproduce the real, but an 'idea' of the real which he has himself created by a process of selection, and which has no exact counterpart in any 'natural object.' The 'end' of Art, therefore, is 'the expression of moral beauty by the assistance of physical beauty.' [1]

In this account of art and genius, Cousin does little more than combine Aristotle's definitions with Plato's doctrine of the essential unity of art and morals. But when he proceeds to describe the idealising process which takes place in the artist's mind—a process identical with Addison's first operation of the imagination—he adds new matter.

'The true artist,' he writes, 'has a profound feeling and admiration for nature; but everything in nature is not equally admirable.' [2] And with Cousin, what Addison had described as 'humouring the imagination in its own notions,' becomes something more definite: it is the unconscious criticism of nature by the human mind, or the process of idealisation. Take a real figure: it will have

[1] So Aristotle says (*Phys.* II. 8, 15) that art, besides 'imitating' nature, also 'completes nature's unfinished designs.' And Hegel similarly places beauty in art above beauty in nature. 'Art,' he says, 'is the highest revelation of the beautiful. Art makes up the deficiencies of natural beauty by bringing the idea into clearer light, by showing the external in its life and spiritual animation.' In respect of the psychological process, Aristotle says that art 'causes all things whereof a "form" exists in the mind to come into being.' The nature of this 'form' is explained in his account of the origin of knowledge (*Analyt. Post.* II. 15, 5). It is the residual notion which remains in the mind after a number of sense-perceptions; and this residual notion is the source (ἀρχή) both of art and science. Conversely, a work of art is the external manifestation of this 'form.' Schelling sums up Aristotle's teaching by the definition of the beautiful in art as 'the shining of the idea through a sensuous medium.' [2] P. 175

some defect which mars its beauty for the senses. But this defect is no obstacle to the mind. In remembering the figure it omits the defect. Take a real action : some details are trivial or sordid ; but the mind can conceive the action without these details. So far the mind selects : but it does more than this. The real figure is deficient in some grace, the real action in some noble trait ; these omissions can be supplied from the store of previous experience. And so by pruning defects and supplying omissions the mind forms an idea, or mental picture, of the figure or action, and it is this idea, and not the particular figure or action, which is presented to us by art. In other words, a work of art is not a representation of a real object, but a representation of a real object in its mental aspect. The prominence given to this mental aspect varies in the several arts ; it is greatest in poetry and least in architecture.

'The end of art is the expression of moral beauty by the assistance of physical beauty. The latter is for art only a symbol of the former. In nature this symbol is often obscure ; art in rendering it clear attains effects which nature does not always produce. Nature has another means of pleasing us, for once again I say she possesses in an incomparable degree that which causes the greatest charm of the imagination and the eyes, life ; art touches us in a higher degree, because, in making the expression of moral beauty its first aim, it appeals more directly to the source of the deepest emotions. Art can be more pathetic than nature, and pathos is the sign and the measure of beauty of the highest class.' [1]

The artist must combine the two elements of the real and the ideal. In so doing he must avoid two equally

[1] P. 176.

dangerous extremes—an ideal that has no life, and the absence of the ideal. The ability to make this delicate adjustment is the sole property of genius. 'Genius,' he writes, 'is a quick and unerring perception of the just proportion in which the ideal and the natural, form and thought, ought to be united. This union is the perfection of art : on these terms the masterpieces are produced.'

It is the necessity for this just relationship between the two elements of the real and the ideal that places illusion, on the one hand, and didactic intention on the other, outside the sphere of art.

If art produces complete illusion, it thereby fails to achieve its proper effect. This effect is lost, for in its place there has arisen a 'perfectly natural and sometimes intolerable feeling.' Such a feeling as caused 'the young Englishman' in witnessing Corneille's tragedy 'to rush sobbing and frantic upon the stage, crying out, "It is Phaedra, it is Phaedra," as though he would have interposed and saved Ariadne.'[1]

Again, though art tends to elevate the soul, it does so indirectly.

'The artist is before all an artist ; what inspires him is the sentiment of beauty ; and the emotion which he wishes to produce in the soul of the spectator is the same as that which fills his own. He trusts to the strength of beauty ; he fortifies it with all the power, with all the charm of the ideal ; it is for beauty to forthwith do its work ; the artist has done his part when he has procured for some chosen spirits the exquisite sense of beauty. This pure and disinterested sentiment is a noble ally of the sentiments of morality and

P. 181: and forward at p. 201.

religion ; it arouses, nourishes, and develops them, but it is a distinct and separate sentiment.' [1]

But in asserting the independence of art Cousin does not intend to dissociate it from morality, religion, and patriotism. 'Art takes its inspirations from these profound sources as well as from the ever-open source of nature,' and ideal beauty is a reflection of the infinite and of God.

'Thus art is in itself essentially moral and religious ; for without being false to its proper law, its proper genius, it everywhere expresses in its works the eternal beauty. Enchained on every side to matter by inflexible bonds, working on an inanimate stone, on vague and fugitive sounds, on words of limited and definite significance, art communicates to them, with the precise form which appeals to this or that sense, a mysterious character which appeals to the imagination and the soul, tears them away from reality and transports them gently or imperiously to unknown regions. Every work of art, whatever be its kind, small or great, expressed in form, song, or speech—every work of art, that is really beautiful or sublime, throws the soul into a gracious or austere dream which raises it towards the infinite. The infinite—there is the common goal to which the soul aspires on the wings of the imagination, as well as on the wings of reason, by the path of the sublime and beautiful as well as by the path of the true and the good. The emotion which beauty produces affects the soul on this side ; it is this beneficent emotion that art procures for humanity.' [2]

And so we approach the second of the two great processes of art. It is nothing else than Addison's second operation of the imagination—the talent of affecting

[1] P. 184.   [2] Pp. 186-7.

the imagination in others. But Cousin finds in an analysis of this process an answer to the fourth question, What separates the Fine Arts? and from this point of view it becomes a presentation of the idea by methods suited to the conditions under which the special arts respectively avail themselves of the several senses. 'All the arts are at one,' he says,[1] 'in their object.' They all strive to express the same thing, 'the idea, the spirit, the soul, the invisible, the infinite. But since in the process of expressing this one and identical thing they address themselves to different senses, this difference in the senses divides art into the different arts.' In other words, natural existences, the play of the elements, and human actions, which together constitute reality and life, are accompanied by certain attributes revealed to us by the senses. But of the five senses, two only, sight and hearing, can directly assist the artist in producing the sentiment of beauty ; and, therefore, art is at once limited to such attributes of reality as are revealed by these two senses ; and the Fine Arts are broadly separated into two classes, the arts of hearing— music and poetry, and the arts of sight—painting, sculpture, and architecture. Such attributes are solidity, form, colour, sound, time, and space. Of these the sculptor takes solidity and form without colour,[2] sound, or time ; and the special subject of his art is physical beauty in repose. The painter has colour, space in line, without solidity, and an appearance of movement without time. His appeal, like the sculptor's, is primarily to the eye ; but the range of this appeal is infinitely extended. The musician has only sound and time ; but with these vague attributes of reality he asserts his dominion over the wide

[1] P. 189. [2] Except in the antiques.

field of the emotions. The poet has neither solidity, form, nor colour, but only time and language with which to effect his representations of the real, and create his images of the actual life around him. Yet so potent, so universal an instrument is language, that the very centre of reality, human life and thought, is the special subject of his art.

Consequently each alike must adopt some special means by which he can hide the deficiencies of his art, and suggest, where he cannot reproduce, reality. This is effected by so emphasising those aspects of his subject which are accompanied by the particular attribute or attributes which he can employ, and subordinating those other aspects which are accompanied by attributes which are not at his command, that the mind is absorbed in perfection and forgets or supplies what is omitted. Hence it follows that in the presentation of the idea a greater or less part of that idea must be regarded as accessory, and must be subordinated to the central motive by the methods respectively appropriate to the several arts. And so, from the point of view of formal criticism, the appeal to the imagination becomes correct composition. And what idealisation is to the artistic function in general, composition is to each special art. It is the presentation of the idea by a method suited to the conditions under which the special art approaches the imagination through the senses. But there is a wide interval between this formal criticism and the formal criticism of the *Poetics*. ' True unity is unity of expression,' he says. ' It is needless to remark that between composition thus understood, and that which is often so named, symmetry and the arrangement of the parts in accordance with artificial rules, there is an abyss. True composition is the most powerful method of expression.'

Freedom of expression is the characteristic of the Fine Arts—the *artes liberales, artes ingenuae,* of antiquity —and by this test Architecture is lowest in the scale, because the architect is most fettered by considerations of utility.[1] But this freedom of expression is controlled by the limits which are in each case fixed by the nature of the means employed. Lessing gave an example of the manner in which Homer expressed the idea of beauty by the true poetic method ; and Cousin, who deals less fully with the methods of the 'arts of sight,' uses Haydn's *Tempest* to show how a master-musician can be no less restrained.

' Give the wisest symphonist a tempest to render. Nothing is easier than to imitate the whistling of the winds and the noise of the thunder. But by what combination of ordered sounds could he present to our sight the lightning flashes which suddenly rend the veil of night, and that which is the most terrific aspect of the tempest, the alternate movement of

[1] This agrees with Hegel's classification of the arts :

1. Architecture	(Sensuous material in excess, but symbolic.)
2. Sculpture .	(An advance towards the ideal as representing the living body.)
3. Painting .	(Eliminates the 3rd dimension of space, and rids itself of the coarse material substrate of sculpture.)
4. Music . .	(The most subjective of the arts—all elements of space are suppressed; its 'content' is the inner emotional nature.)
5. Poetry .	(Has privilege of universal expression; it contains all other arts in itself, namely, the plastic art in the epic, music in the ode, and the unity of both in the drama.)

the waves, now rising mountain high, now sinking and seeming to fall headlong into bottomless abysses? If the hearer has not been told beforehand what the subject is, he will never divine it, and I defy him to distinguish a tempest from a battle.   In spite of scientific skill and genius, sounds cannot represent forms.   Music, rightly advised, will refuse to enter upon a hopeless contest; it will not undertake to express the rise and fall of the waves and other like phenomena; it will do better: with sounds it will produce in our soul the feelings which successively arise in us during the various scenes of the tempest.   It is thus that Haydn will become the rival, even the conqueror of the painter, because it has been given to music to move and sway the soul even more profoundly than painting.' [1]

At the other end of the scale is poetry, which is least dependent upon the senses, and, therefore, most expressive.   By means of language it can appeal directly to the soul through the imagination.

'Speech is the instrument of poetry; poetry moulds it to its uses and idealises it that so it may express ideal beauty.   It gives it the charm and majesty of metre, it turns it into something that is neither voice nor music, but which partakes of the nature of both, something at once material and spiritual, something finished, clear, and precise, like the sharpest contours and form, something living and animated like colour, something pathetic and infinite like sound.   A word in itself, above all a word chosen and transfigured by poetry is the most energetic and the most universal of symbols.   Equipped with this talisman of its own creation poetry reflects all the images of the world of the senses, like sculpture and painting; reflects feeling like painting and music, rendering it in all its variations—variations which

[1] Pp. 195–6.

music cannot reach, and that come in a rapid succession which painting cannot follow, while it remains as sharply turned and as full of repose as sculpture; nor is that all, it expresses what is inaccessible to all other arts, I mean thought, thought which has no colour, thought which allows no sound to escape, which is revealed in no play of feature, thought in its loftiest flight, in its most refined abstraction.' [1]

In this recognition of words as the supreme instrument for arousing the imagination, and of 'thought' as the supreme element in poetry, we have returned through the various analyses of formal criticism to the standpoint which Addison adopted. And it is from this standpoint of thought, not form—of poetry as the highest expression of the imaginative reason—that criticism to-day looks out upon all creative literature.

[1] Pp. 202-3.

CHAPTER VIII

MATTHEW ARNOLD INSISTS UPON THE INTERPRETATIVE
POWER OF LITERATURE : THE 'HIGH SERIOUSNESS
OF ABSOLUTE SINCERITY' IS THE TEST OF SUPREME
MERIT IN POETRY

MATTHEW ARNOLD is not merely a critic of letters : he
is a critic of life also. He identifies the literature of a
period with the life of that period, and equally his criticism
of literature proceeds upon the same lines as his criticism
of life. And there is this that is remarkable in his position. He is a critic in an epoch of criticism, a reformer
in an age of reform—a critic of the critics and a reformer
of the reformers. The very titles of his works have
a challenging ring : *God and the Bible, Literature and
Dogma, Culture and Anarchy.* The man who assumes
this attitude is obliged to emphasise and exaggerate the
points on which he conceives that he differs from his
contemporaries. And for this purpose Matthew Arnold
brings all life to the test of the ideal. Nothing will
satisfy him short of perfection. Even where he admits
that the ideal cannot be attained, he insists upon the
necessity of keeping it in view, for future improvement
depends upon the recognition of present imperfection.
'Perfection,' he says,[1] 'can never be reached without
seeing things as they really are.' Neither politicians, nor

[1] *Culture and Anarchy,* Pref. p. xxxiv.

theologians, nor even the poets could do this, he thought ; and, therefore, he suggested a remedy, a means of 'seeing things as they really are.' The whole scope of his essay *Culture and Anarchy* is 'to recommend culture as the great help out of our present difficulties ; culture being a pursuit of our total perfection by means of getting to know, on all matters which most concern us, the best that has been thought and said in the world ; and through this knowledge, turning a stream of fresh and free thought upon our stock notions and habits, which we now follow staunchly but mechanically.' [1]

What Matthew Arnold here calls 'culture' is something which is more properly indicated by the term 'criticism.' He speaks of this remedy as a 'pursuit' and a 'getting to know,' implying a certain progress and activity which is alien to the idea of culture. For culture is rather the mental condition which results from the possession of knowledge, whereas what Arnold recommends is plainly the acquisition of this mental condition by distinguishing truth from falsehood—that is, by criticism. In other words, he here states as a process what is in reality *the result* of that process. And subsequently we find that he himself identifies 'culture' with 'criticism.' The business of criticism, he writes [2] in his essay on the *Function of Criticism at the Present Time*, 'is, as I have said, simply to know the best that is known and thought in the world, and by in its turn making this known, to create a current of true and fresh ideas.' And the essential quality of criticism is 'disinterestedness.' 'Its business,' he continues, 'is to do this with inflexible honesty, with due ability ; but its business is to

[1] Ib., p. viii.   [2] *Essays in Criticism*, I. p. 18.

do no more, and to leave alone all questions of practical consequences and applications, questions which will never fail to have due prominence given to them.'

Now, in this identification of culture with criticism we have an example of what is a characteristic of his thought, as it was of Addison's thought. I mean the gradual advance in the direction of definiteness shown by his later, as compared with his earlier writings. This will, I hope, become apparent, even in the necessarily limited account of the one aspect of that thought—literary criticism—which is here offered to the reader.

Matthew Arnold finds a starting-point for his criticism in his knowledge of the literature of ancient Greece. But in so doing he has more than one advantage over Addison. Apart from a more accurate knowledge of the Greek language and of Greek authors, he takes the literature first and the theory, as given in the *Poetics*, afterwards. And he subsequently finds another starting-point in his knowledge of continental literature. In this way he approaches the study of English literature from two separate points of view, and finally he acquires that independence, that detachment from local and his-torical interests, which is the crowning merit of a critic ; for comparison is the life-blood of criticism. But, as I said, he starts from a knowledge of Greek literature.

The difference between Greek and modern poetry he finds to be a difference of construction.

' The radical difference between their poetical theory and ours consists, as it appears to me, in this : that, with them, the poetical character of an action in itself and the conduct of it was the first consideration ; with us, attention is fixed mainly on the value of the separate thoughts and images which occur in the treatment of an action. They regarded the whole; we regard the parts.' [1]

The deficiency of construction, which he finds characteristic of contemporary poetry, he attributes to the absorption of the age in scientific pursuits. For discovery produces an analytic tendency of mind; whereas the tendency of mind which is helpful to the artist is synthetic.

'The grand work of literary genius is a work of synthesis and exposition, not of analysis and discovery; its gift lies in the faculty of being happily inspired by a certain intellectual and spiritual atmosphere, by a certain order of ideas, when it finds itself in them; of dealing divinely with these ideas, presenting them in the most effective and attractive combinations— making beautiful works with them, in short.' [2]

And, therefore, the present age was, in his opinion, one in which any great manifestation of creative genius was not to be expected.

'Poets are told that it is an era of progress, an age commissioned to carry out the great ideas of industrial development and social amelioration. They reply that with all this they can do nothing; that the elements they need for the exercise of their art are great actions calculated powerfully and delightfully to affect what is permanent in the human soul; that so far as the present age can supply such actions they will gladly make use of them; but that an age wanting in moral grandeur can with difficulty supply such, and an age of spiritual discomfort with difficulty be powerfully and delightfully affected by them.' [3]

[1] *Irish Essays*, Pref. to Poems, p. 288.
[2] *Essays in Criticism*, I. p. 5.   [3] *Irish Essays*, p. 302.

Afterwards, however, he suggests a further difference between Greek and modern poetry, which is to the advantage not of the Greek, but of the modern poets.

'The poetry of later paganism lived by the senses and understanding; the poetry of mediæval Christianity lived by the heart and imagination. But the main element of the modern spirit's life is neither the senses and understanding, nor the heart and imagination; it is the imaginative reason. And there is a century in Greek life—the century preceding the Peloponnesian War, from about the year 530 to the year 430 B.C.—in which poetry made, it seems to me, the noblest, the most successful effort she has ever made as the priestess of the imaginative reason, of the element by which the modern spirit, if it would live right, has chiefly to live. Of this effort, of which the four great names are Simonides, Pindar, Æschylus, Sophocles, I must not now attempt more than the bare mention. . . . No doubt that effort was imperfect. Perhaps everything, take it at what point in its existence you will, carries within itself the fatal law of its own ulterior development. Perhaps, even of the life of Pindar's time, Pompeii was the inevitable bourne. Perhaps the life of their beautiful Greece could not afford to its poets all that fulness of varied experience, all that power of emotion, which

> ". . . the heavy and the weary weight
> Of all this unintelligible world"

affords the poet of after-times. Perhaps in Sophocles the thinking-power a little overbalances the religious sense, as in Dante the religious sense overbalances the thinking-power. The present has to make its own poetry, and not even Sophocles and his compeers, any more than Dante and Shakspeare, are enough for it.' [1]

[1] *Essays in Criticism*, I. pp. 220-1.

And in his final account of poetry, he decides that the 'high seriousness' which is the mark of supreme poetic merit belongs to Dante, Shakespeare, and Milton as much as to Homer and Sophocles.

Moreover, he modifies the disparaging estimate which he originally formed of contemporary poetry, as based upon his estimate of the character of contemporary life.

It seemed to him that in such an age poetry and literature must be critical, not creative. But criticism subsequently comes to mean for him all that is best and most characteristic of poetry. There are two orders in literature, he says,[1] 'the famous men of genius—the Homers, Dantes, Shakspeares,' and 'the famous men of ability'; but the work of these two orders ' is at the bottom the same—a criticism of life. The end and aim of all literature, if one considers it attentively, is, in truth, nothing but that.' As a matter of fact, while Arnold was complaining of the materialism of the age, a great poetic literature was growing up, which included, together with his own work, that of Tennyson, Browning, D. G. Rossetti, Swinburne, William Morris, and George Meredith.[2] The lack of ideas, which he attributed to the sterility of the Victorian epoch, was really the result of its youth. The happy concurrence of 'the power of the man and the power of the moment' did, in fact, come while his thoughts were still fixed upon the past. And for that reason he has only a dim consciousness of the

[1] Ib., p. 303.
[2] And what would he have said of Mr. Rudyard Kipling? Surely in Mr. Kipling's verse we have an example of Emerson's new art—the art which raises to a divine use the railroad, the galvanic battery, and the ' primary assemblies '—in short, all the applications of science, and all the manifestations of social and political progress.

change. 'I grant,'[1] he says, 'it is mainly the privilege of faith, at present, to discern this end to our railways, our business, and our fortune-making ; but we shall see if, here as elsewhere, faith is not in the end the true prophet.' And he concludes his essay on the Function of Criticism—the instrument by which the new order of thought was to be brought into being—with these words :

'The epochs of Æschylus and Shakspeare make us feel their pre-eminence. In an epoch like those is, no doubt, the true life of literature ; there is the promised land, towards which criticism can only beckon. That promised land it will not be ours to enter, and we shall die in the wilderness : but to have desired to enter it, to have saluted it from afar, is already, perhaps, the best distinction among contemporaries ; it will certainly be the best title to esteem with posterity.'[2]

If he had only known it, he was not in the wilderness when he died.

But this dim consciousness of the change which was going on around him was sufficient to enable him to distinguish between the character of the possible harvest of the future and that of the early nineteenth-century poetry—the work of Shelley, Keats, Scott, Coleridge, Byron, and Wordsworth. And he tells us very definitely to what the failure of this poetry was due. It was due to an absence of ideas in the nation at large.

'We in England, in our great burst of literature during the first thirty years of the present century, had no manifestation of the modern spirit, as this spirit manifests itself in Goethe's works or Heine's. And the reason is not far to seek. We had neither the German wealth of ideas, nor the French enthusiasm for applying ideas. There reigned in

[1] Ib., p. 17.   [2] Ib., p. 41.

the mass of the nation that inveterate inaccessibility to ideas, that Philistinism—to use the German nickname—which reacts even on the individual genius that is exempt from it.' [1]

And so Byron and Shelley 'did not succeed in their attempt freely to apply the modern spirit in English literature ; . . . the resistance to baffle them, the want of intelligent sympathy to guide and uphold them were too great.' Without this application of the modern spirit—that is to say, the identification of the poet with the life of his epoch—what he writes loses the poetic quality of universality, and becomes only partial truth. Even the external circumstances of his life are affected. This was the case with Wordsworth, who 'retired into a monastery' ; with Coleridge, ' who took opium ' ; with Scott, 'who became the historiographer-royal of feudalism' ; with Keats, 'who died of consumption at twenty-five.'

' Wordsworth, Scott, and Keats have left admirable works ; far more solid and complete works than those which Byron and Shelley have left. But their works have this defect— they do not belong to that which is the main current of the literature of modern epochs, they do not apply modern ideas to life ; they constitute, therefore, *minor currents,* and all other literary work of our day, however popular, which has the same defect, also constitutes but a minor current.' [2]

These extracts serve to give us some idea of the general standpoint from which Arnold looks out upon contemporary life, and also of his method of approaching the study of literature, and we are, therefore, now in a position to examine more at length the actual contribution which he has made to the science and practice of literary criticism.

[1] Ib., p. 175.   [2] Ib., p. 177.

But, first, it will be well for me to indicate at once what I conceive to be the sum of the advance which is embodied in his writings on this subject. It is this. The test of symmetry which was laid down by Aristotle in the *Poetics* was found by Addison to be inadequate, and a new test, that of the power to appeal to the imagination, was substituted in its place. The former was a material test, and its use implied that the form of literature was prior in importance to the thought : the latter is a spiritual test, and its use implies that the thought of literature has been recognised as prior in importance to its form.

In what respects, then, has Arnold advanced ? In the first place, he has *applied* this principle to the study of literature. Addison only discovered it after he had tried to measure *Paradise Lost* by the rules of formal criticism. But it is from this aspect—thought, not form —that Matthew Arnold wrote of poetry and poets from the first.

'The grand power of poetry is its interpretative power . . . it interprets by expressing with magical felicity the physiognomy and movement of the outward world, and it interprets by expressing with inspired conviction the ideas and laws of the inward world of man's moral and spiritual nature.' [1]

In the next place, he gave definiteness to the principle by pointing out that there was a special field of the imagination which belonged to poetry as of right ; and that poetry of the highest order confined itself to appealing to the imagination within this sphere.

[1] Ib., p. 110.

'We should conceive of poetry,' he says in his essay on the *Study of Poetry*, 'more worthily and more highly than it has been the custom to conceive of it. We should conceive of it as capable of higher uses, and called to higher destinies, than those which in general men have assigned to it hitherto. More and more mankind will discover that we have to turn to poetry to interpret life for us, to console us, to sustain us.' [1]

Under such a conception as this, the test of poetic excellence can no longer be solely a talent for affecting the imagination, still less a perfectly constructed plot ; it becomes a moral accent.

'For supreme poetical success,' he continues, 'more is required than the powerful application of ideas to life ; it must be an application under the conditions fixed by the laws of poetic truth and poetic beauty. Those laws fix as an essential condition, in the poet's treatment of such matters as are here in question, high seriousness—the high seriousness which comes from absolute sincerity.' [2]

Here in respect of poetry at least we have a conception in which thought and form, truth and beauty, are as intimately connected as they were in the ideal commonwealth of Plato.

> '. . . the truth which draws
> Through all things upwards—that a twofold world
> Must go to a perfect cosmos.   Natural things
> And spiritual—who separates those two
> In art, in morals, or the social drift,
> Tears up the bond of nature and brings death,
> Paints futile pictures, writes unreal verse,
> Leads vulgar days, deals ignorantly with men,
> Is wrong, in short, at all points.' [3]

1 Ib., Second Series, p. 2.   2 Ib., p. 48.
3 *Aurora Leigh*, Bk. VII.

The new principles which Matthew Arnold has introduced into the study of literature can be grouped, I
think, under one or other of the following propositions :

I. The action of two distinct factors can be traced in
any work of creative literature—the personality of the
author, and the mental atmosphere of the age.

II. Poetic thought can be presented in prose or verse,
and the only limit to structural freedom is the natural
requirement that the form of the vehicle should be
appropriate to the character of the thought conveyed.

III. Poetry is a 'criticism of life' : its subject-matter
embraces not only human action, but all conscious manifestations of human activity, including thought not merely
as 'sentiment'—*i.e.* the thought which precedes or conditions action ; but thought as the depository of the
mental experience and the spiritual aspirations of the
race.

IV. As a branch of art, poetry is characterised by its
'interpretative power' : its truth, as compared with the
truth of science, is the truth of feeling, not the truth of
signs, and the test of supreme poetic merit is the 'high
seriousness of absolute sincerity'—a quality which pre-
supposes the morality of the poet.

Matthew Arnold exhibits the essential connection
between the artist and his age—which corresponds to
the scientific analysis of thinking man into the 'organism'
and the 'social medium'[1]—in two ways. In the first
place, to form a great epoch of literature the power of
the man and the power of the moment must be present
in conjunction ; and in the second, either of these

[1] G. H. Lewes' *Problems of Life and Mind.*

powers alone and by itself produces failure, that is, partial success. Genius alone is not sufficient; it must have a certain atmosphere and

'find itself amidst a certain order of ideas, in order to work freely. . . . This is why great creative epochs in literature are so rare, this is why there is so much that is unsatisfactory in the productions of many men of real genius; because, for the creation of a master-work of literature two powers must concur, the power of the man and the power of the moment.' [1]

And again,

'In the Greece of Pindar and Sophocles, in the England of Shakspeare, the poet lived in a current of ideas in the highest degree animating and nourishing to the creative power; society was, in the fullest measure, permeated by fresh thought, intelligent and alive.'

But,

'In the England of the first quarter of this century there was neither a national glow of life and thought, such as we had in the age of Elizabeth, nor yet a culture and a force of learning and criticism such as were to be found in Germany. Therefore the creative power of poetry wanted, for success in the highest sense, materials and a basis; a thorough interpretation of the world was necessarily denied to it.'

If the power of the moment is present without the power of the man, we get a Heine. In Heine's works 'the main current of German literature after Goethe' flowed: he was himself powerfully touched by the modern spirit, 'the sense of want of correspondence between the forms of modern Europe and its spirit, between the new wine of the eighteenth and nineteenth

[1] *Essays in Criticism*, I. p. 5.

centuries and the old bottles of the eleventh and twelfth centuries.' He had the German wealth of ideas to provide him with a suitable atmosphere, but he was defective in the element of personality. 'To his intellectual deliverance there was an addition of something else wanting, and that something else was something immense ; the old-fashioned, laborious, eternally needful moral deliverance.' And, therefore, Arnold pronounces the judgment of partial success upon him.

'Heine had all the culture of Germany ; in his head fermented all the ideas of modern Europe. And what have we got from Heine? A half-result, for want of moral balance, and of nobleness of soul and character.' [1]

If the power of the man is present without the power of the moment, we get a Byron or a Gray. In the case of Byron we have to strike a balance between the gain which arises from his personality, ' the splendid and imperishable excellence of sincerity and strength,' [2] and the defects which arise from his ignorance of life, and make him, in Goethe's words, 'a child, the moment he reflects.' [3]

'Look at Byron, that Byron whom the present generation of Englishmen are forgetting ; Byron, the greatest natural force, the greatest elementary power, I cannot but think, which has appeared in our literature since Shakespeare.[4] And what became of this wonderful production of nature? He shattered himself, he inevitably shattered himself to

---

[1] Ib., p. 193.

[2] Mr. Swinburne's phrase, which Arnold adopts.

[3] Ib., II. p. 202 and p. 185.

[4] The spelling of 'Shakespeare' is varied as above in the 'second series' of Essays.

pieces against the huge, black, cloud-topped, interminable precipice of British Philistinism.' [1]

Gray, the one classic poet of the eighteenth century, had ' knowledge, penetration, seriousness, sentiment, humour . . . the equipment and endowment for the office of poet,' but he fell upon an age of prose. For want of the appropriate mental atmosphere his genius was cursed with sterility, ' he never spoke out in poetry.'

' Gray, with the qualities of mind and soul of a genuine poet, was isolated in his century. Maintaining and fortifying them by lofty studies, he yet could not fully educe and enjoy them ; the want of a genial atmosphere, the failure of sympathy in his contemporaries, were too great. Born in the same year with Milton, Gray would have been another man ; born in the same year with Burns, he would have been another man. A man born in 1608 could profit by the larger and more poetic scope of the English spirit in the Elizabethan age ; a man born in 1759 could profit by that European renewing of men's minds of which the great historical manifestation is the French Revolution.' [2]

Since these two elements, the age and the man, are present in all forms of creative literature, it follows that it is part of the duty of a critic to ascertain the varying degrees in which they respectively affect a particular author or a particular work. The poet, it has been well said, is like a river, which returns in a clear stream the moisture which it has received in vapour from the country through which it passes. The extent, therefore, to which this return is made affords one basis at least upon which the merit of a particular author can be

[1] Ib., I. p. 192.　　　　[2] Ib., II. p. 92.

estimated. But in order to apply this test the critic must have an independent knowledge of the life and thought of the epoch to which the author belongs. And therefore Matthew Arnold writes, in his criticism of Heine, that 'to ascertain the master current in the literature of an epoch, and to distinguish this from all minor currents, is one of the critic's highest functions.' Heine's work did embody the master-current of his epoch, and therefore he ranks as a European poet. Wordsworth and Byron embodied only side-currents, and for that reason they must be placed lower in merit than Heine. In the case of contemporary writers it is the fact that time must elapse before the master-current of the age can be distinguished, that creates the chief difficulty in judging of their several merits with any degree of certainty.

The clearest evidence of the extent to which Arnold accepts prose as a vehicle of poetic thought is afforded by the circumstance that his most valuable account of the character of that thought arises out of a consideration of the prose writings of Maurice de Guérin. I shall presently refer to this account, and therefore I need only say here that Matthew Arnold finds that 'intimate sense of objects' which is characteristic of the interpretations of poetry, in the prose of Chateaubriand, of Senancour, and especially in the prose compositions of Maurice de Guérin.[1] From the theoretic point of view there is nothing new in this identification of prose and verse. Aristotle identified them, and so did Bacon. But I know of no other writer on criticism who has gone to a prose composition to illustrate not merely a

[1] Ib., I. p. 82.

characteristic merit, but *the* characteristic merit of poetic thought.

In other respects he adds to our knowledge by defining and contrasting the respective characteristics of both. English prose reached its maturity in the eighteenth century—our 'excellent and indispensable' eighteenth century, our 'age of prose and reason,' of which Dryden was the 'puissant and glorious founder,' and Pope 'the splendid high priest.'

'The needful qualities for a fit prose are regularity, uniformity, precision, balance. The men of letters, whose destiny it may be to bring their nation to the attainment of a fit prose, must of necessity, whether they work in prose or in verse, give a predominating, an almost exclusive attention to the qualities of regularity, uniformity, precision, balance. But an almost exclusive attention to these qualities involves some repression and silencing of poetry.' [1]

As an example he takes a sentence from Dryden :

'What Virgil wrote in the vigour of his age, in plenty and at ease, I have undertaken to translate in my declining years; struggling with wants, oppressed by sickness, curbed in my genius, liable to be misconstrued in all I write.'

And in his essay on the *Literary Influence of Academies*, he decides that England is weak in prose.

'Our literature, in spite of the genius manifested in it, may fall short in form, method, precision, proportions, arrangement—all of them, I have said, things where intelligence proper comes in. It may be comparatively weak in prose, that branch of literature where intelligence proper is, so to speak, all in all. In this branch it may show many

[1] Ib., II. p. 39.

grave faults to which the want of a quick, flexible intelligence, and of the strict standard which such an intelligence tends to impose, makes it liable; it may be full of hap-hazard crudeness, provincialism, eccentricity, violence, blundering. It may be a less stringent and effective intellectual agency, both upon our own nation and upon the world at large, than other literatures which show less genius, perhaps, but more intelligence.' [1]

On the other hand, England is strong in poetry; and the pre-eminence of the English poets is due, in part to the presence of an underlying morality, and in part to the possession of a vehicle, blank verse, which nearly approaches prose in respect of perfect freedom. The English poets, he says, answer the question, *How to live ?*

'Voltaire was right in thinking that the energetic and profound treatment of moral ideas, in this large sense, is what distinguishes the English poetry. He sincerely meant praise, not dispraise or hint of limitation; and they err who suppose that poetic limitation is a necessary consequence of the fact, the fact being granted as Voltaire states it. If what distinguishes the greatest poets is their powerful and profound application of ideas to life, which surely no good critic will deny, then to prefix to the term "ideas" here the term "moral" makes hardly any difference, because human life itself is in so preponderating a degree moral.' [2]

And therefore, he adds, that to say that the English poets are remarkable in dealing with moral ideas 'is only another way of saying that in poetry the English genius has especially shown its power.'

And English poets have an advantage over the French in respect of their poetic vehicle.

[1] Ib., I. p. 55.   [2] Ib., II. p. 143.

'In prose the character of the vehicle for the composer's thoughts is not determined beforehand; every composer has to make his own vehicle; and who has ever done this more admirably than the great prose writers of France—Pascal, Bossuet, Fénélon, Voltaire? But in verse the composer has (with comparatively narrow limit of modification) to accept his vehicle ready-made; it is therefore of vital importance to him that he should find at his disposal a vehicle adequate to convey the highest matters of poetry. We may even get a decisive test of the poetical power of a language and nation by ascertaining how far the principal poetical vehicle which they have employed, how far (in plainer words) the established national metre for high poetry, is adequate or inadequate. It seems to me that the established metre of this kind in France—the Alexandrine—is inadequate; that as a vehicle for high poetry it is greatly inferior to the hexameter or to the iambics of Greece (for example), or to the blank verse of England. Therefore, . . . Racine is at a disadvantage as compared with Sophocles or Shakespeare, and he is likewise at a disadvantage as compared with Bossuet.' [1]

And in his essay on Wordsworth he quotes some remarks of M. Henri Cochin which support his contention.

' "With Shakespeare," he says, "prose comes in whenever the subject, being more familiar, is unsuited to the majestic English iambic." And he goes on: "Shakespeare is the king of poetic rhythm and style, as well as the king of the realm of thought; along with his dazzling prose, Shakespeare has succeeded in giving us the most varied, the most harmonious verse which has ever sounded upon the human ear since the verse of the Greeks." ' [2]

[1] Ib., I. p. 83; and see Note (4) on p. 148 *supra*.
[2] Ib., II. p. 130.

And in the same essay there is a useful passage on the classification of poetic forms.

'We may rely upon it that we shall not improve upon the classification adopted by the Greeks for kinds of poetry; that their categories of epic, dramatic, lyric, and so forth, have a natural propriety, and should be adhered to. It may sometimes seem doubtful to which of two categories a poem belongs; whether this or that poem is to be called, for instance, narrative or lyric, lyric or elegiac. But there is to be found in every good poem a strain, a predominant note, which determines the poem as belonging to one of these kinds rather than the other; and here is the best proof of the value of the classification, and of the advantage of adhering to it.' [1]

When Matthew Arnold calls poetry a 'criticism of life,' he uses a form of words which, more than any other phrase, embodies the modern conception of poetry. As a criticism of life poetry includes all that is most important in the opinions of men, expressed with the highest degree of lucidity and the utmost beauty of language and idea. Only those opinions which have become effective by being assimilated into the moral constitution of man, are embodied and presented by poetry. It rejects the crudities of science in which the logic of signs has as yet no basis in the logic of feeling.

Being concerned with the facts of life it is essentially moral.

'It is important, therefore, to hold fast to this: that poetry is at bottom a criticism of life; that the greatness of a poet lies in his powerful and beautiful application of ideas to life—to the question: How to live. Morals are often treated in a narrow and false fashion; they are bound up with systems of thought and

[1] Ib., p. 137.

belief which have had their day; they are fallen into the hands of pedants and professional dealers; they grow tiresome to some of us. We find attraction, at times, even in a poetry of revolt against them; in a poetry which might take for its motto Omar Kheyam's words: "Let us make up in the tavern for the time which we have wasted in the mosque." Or we find attractions in a poetry indifferent to them; in a poetry where the contents may be what they will, but where the form is studied and exquisite. We delude ourselves in either case; and the best cure for our delusion is to let our minds rest upon that great and inexhaustible word *life*, until we learn to enter into its meaning. A poetry of revolt against moral ideas is a poetry of revolt against *life*; a poetry of indifference towards moral ideas is a poetry of indifference towards *life*.' [1]

Rejecting all opinions except those that have become part of the moral constitution of mankind, the best poetry becomes in an increasing degree a depository for the most assured experience, and since we project ourselves into the future by means of our knowledge of the past, of the most assured aspirations of the race. In poetry, therefore, where 'the idea is everything,' the race will find 'an ever surer and surer stay.' The object of poetry thus conceived is to produce neither pleasurable emotion nor intellectual enjoyment. It has a higher mission: it has to bring man into harmony with life, to explain life to him, to tell him how to live.

'Without poetry our science will appear incomplete; and most of what passes with us for religion and philosophy will be replaced by poetry. Science, I say, will appear incomplete without it. For finely and truly does Wordsworth call poetry "the impassioned expression which is in the countenance of all science;" and what is a countenance without its ex-

[1] Ib., p. 143.

pression ? Again, Wordsworth finely and truly calls poetry "the breath and finer spirit of all knowledge : " our religion, parading evidences such as those on which the popular mind relies now ; our philosophy, pluming itself on its reasonings about causation and finite and infinite being ; what are they but the shadows and dreams and false shows of knowledge ? The day will come when we shall wonder at ourselves for having trusted to them, for having taken them seriously ; and the more we perceive their hollowness, the more we shall prize "the breath and finer spirit of knowledge" offered to us by poetry.' [1]

But it remains to explain how it is that poetry can tell us more of life than science.

It uses, in common with the other fine arts, the idealising process of art, but it uses this process in a higher degree than any of its fellows. And therefore the 'grand power' of poetry as an art is its 'interpretative power.' It interprets, of course, by means of words and ideas, but how does it differ in its use of words and ideas from science ? What makes it, as Wordsworth says, the *finer spirit* of all knowledge ?

It is in the answer which Matthew Arnold gives to this question that his merit as a critic is most conspicuous. For the purpose of exhibiting this merit in a clear light let me first place before the reader the answer which Wordsworth himself gives. In the 'Observations' in which he uses this expression he proceeds :

'The sum of what I have said is, that the poet is chiefly distinguished from other men by a greater promptness to think and feel without immediate external excitement, and a greater power in expressing such thoughts and feelings as are produced in him

[1] Ib., p. 3.

in that manner. But these passions and thoughts and feelings are the general passions and thoughts and feelings of men. And with what are they connected? Undoubtedly with our moral sentiments and animal sensations, and with the causes which excite these. . . . The poet thinks and feels in the spirit of the passions of men. How, then, can his language differ in any material degree from that of all other men who feel vividly and see clearly? . . . *He must express himself as other men express themselves.*'

Why then has Wordsworth written in verse?

Because, he replies, he has restricted himself to the subjects of poetry : the 'great and universal passions of men, the most general and interesting of their occupations, and the entire world of nature.' He continues :

'Now, supposing for a moment that whatever is interesting in these objects may be as vividly described in prose, why am I to be condemned, if to such description I have endeavoured to superadd the charm which, by the consent of all nations, is acknowledged to exist in metrical language!'

And he then adds that the charm of metrical composition consists in the fact, that the excitement, which passionate words and images would produce in the mind of the reader, is tempered by the regularity and restraint of the vehicle in which they are presented.

Accepting for the moment this account of the effect of metre—which is quite opposed to the view stated above, that the greatness of poetry is in proportion to the freedom of the poet from metrical restraint—this explanation at best only tells us why poetic thought is more *agreeable :* it does not tell us why it is more *convincing,* why it is the *finer* spirit, the essence of knowledge.

On the other hand, Arnold writes with precision : its

increased clearness is due to the fact that it uses the logic of feeling as well as the logic of signs.

'The grand power of poetry is its interpretative power; by which I mean, not a power of drawing out in black and white an explanation of the mystery of the universe, but the power of so dealing with things as to awaken in us a wonderfully full, new, and intimate sense of them, and of our relations with them. When this sense is awakened in us as to objects without us, we feel ourselves to be in contact with the essential nature of those objects, to be no longer bewildered and oppressed by them, but to have their secret, and to be in harmony with them; and this feeling calms and satisfies us as no other can.[1]   Poetry, indeed, interprets in another way besides this; but one of its two ways of interpreting, of exercising its highest power, is by awakening this sense in us.   I will not now inquire whether this sense is illusive, whether it can be proved not to be illusive, whether it does absolutely make us possess the real nature of things; all I say is, that poetry can awaken it in us, and that to awaken it is one of the highest powers of poetry.   The interpretations of science do not give us this intimate sense of objects as the interpretations of poetry give it; *they appeal to a limited faculty, and not to the whole man.*[2]   It is not Linnæus or Cavendish or Cuvier who gives us the true sense of animals, or water, or plants, who seizes their secret for us, who makes us participate in their life; it is Shakspeare, with his

> " daffodils
> That come before the swallow dares, and take
> The winds of March with beauty; "

it is Wordsworth, with his

> " Voice . . . heard
> In spring-time from the cuckoo-bird,

[1] This feeling appears throughout his poetry, but perhaps most in *Self-Dependence*.

[2] The italics are not in the original.

> Breaking the silence of the seas
> Among the farthest Hebrides ; "

it is Keats, with his

> " Moving waters at their priest-like task
> Of cold ablution round Earth's human shores ; "

it is Chateaubriand with his " *cîme indéterminée des forêts ;* "
it is Senancour, with his mountain birch-tree : " *Cette écorce
blanche, lisse et crevassée ; cette tige agreste ; ces branches qui
s'inclinent vers la terre ; la mobilité des feuilles, et tout cet abandon,
simplicité de la nature, attitude des déserts.*" ' [1]

And again :

'Poetry is interpretative both by having *natural magic* in it,
and by having *moral profundity*. In both ways it illuminates
man ; it gives him a satisfying sense of reality ; it reconciles
him with himself and the universe. Thus Æschylus's "δράσαντι
παθεῖν " and his " ἀνήριθμον γέλασμα " are alike interpretative.
Shakspeare interprets both when he says,

> " Full many a glorious morning have I seen,
> Flatter the mountain-tops with sovran eye ; "

and when he says,

> " There's a divinity that shapes our ends,
> Rough-hew them as we will."

These great poets unite in themselves the faculty of both kinds
of interpretation, the naturalistic and the moral. But it is
observable that in the poets who unite both kinds, the latter
(the moral) usually ends by making itself the master. In
Shakspeare the two kinds seems wonderfully to balance one
another ; but even in him the balance leans ; his expression
tends to become too little sensuous and simple, too much
intellectualised.' [2]

[1] Ib., I. p. 81.   [2] Ib., p. 111.

The power of poetry is its interpretative power, the object upon which it works is life, and it follows, therefore, that the test of poetic merit is 'truth.' For this is the sole test by which the possession of this power can be measured. But 'to poetic truth of substance, in its natural and necessary union with poetic truth of style,' must be added 'the high seriousness which comes from absolute sincerity.' This is the accent which marks supreme poetical success, the accent of the masters.

For Matthew Arnold's conception of poetry is not merely a conception, an ideal; it is an actual estimate. Here, in literature at least, he was able to find that perfection in the pursuit of which he spent his life. If we ask, How can this accent be detected? Where can this perfect poetry be found? he replies, as Addison had done before him, that all lesser poetry must be brought to the touchstone of the masters—Homer, Dante, Shakespeare, Milton. And he himself joyfully recognises this accent in the very poets whom Plato so grievously misunderstood. For of the Greek poets he writes:

'No other poets have lived so much by the imaginative reason; no other poets have made their work so well balanced; no other poets, who have so well satisfied the thinking-power, have so well satisfied the religious sense.' [1]

It is in this increased power of appreciation that the development of criticism is most conspicuously seen. We may set on one side Plato's examination of Greek poetry, as nullified by the severity of the ideal tests which he adopted; but how cold and restrained does Aristotle's approval of Sophocles and Homer appear by the side of

[1] Ib., p. 222.

Addison's enthusiastic recognition of the beauties of Milton. And the difference between the Greek and the modern estimate of poetry becomes still more apparent, when we compare the language of Plato and Aristotle with the familiar, almost caressing, accents which contemporary English authors have taught us to associate with any criticism of poetry. There is Ruskin's assertion of the essential morality which underlies the artist nature, ' All right human song is the finished expression by art, of the joy or grief of noble persons, for right causes ; ' Arnold's sad promise of the future, ' In poetry our race will find an ever surer and surer stay ; ' Emerson's quick recognition of its perpetual vitality, ' When the poet sings, the world listens with the assurance that now a secret of God is to be spoken.'

And why this change from formal analysis to reverent appreciation ? Is it not because the common thought of man has drawn nearer to that finer and more spiritual perception of things which has characterised poetry from the very first ?

CHAPTER IX

THE INTERPRETATIVE POWER OF POETRY—IT INTERPRETS
HUMAN ACTION, NATURE, STATES OF MIND, INDIVI-
DUAL AND COLLECTIVE

IMITATION, Representation, Interpretation : in these
three words we have the history of our conception of
poetry. The aims which these words embody are found
in all forms of poetry, but they are manifested in varying
degrees ; and the relative degrees of prominence which
they severally attain define broadly certain stages in the
growth of poetry, or creative literature, as a whole. To-
day, the last aim is dominant, and the 'grand power of
poetry' is felt to be its 'interpretative power.'

After all it is doubtful whether we can obtain a better
or clearer perception of the real nature of this interpretative power than we do from Addison.

Addison makes the power of poetry and the Fine Arts
consist in the appeal to the imagination ; makes poetry
avail itself of this appeal more than any other art : and he
points out the twofold use of the faculty of the imagination which is involved in the process. There is not
only the working of the imaginative reason in the poet's
mind, but there is the working of the imaginative reason
in the mind of the hearer or reader. In this latter operation our own mind co-operates with the mind of the
poet, and it is this co-operation which makes poetry give

us the intimate sense of the reality of things of which Matthew Arnold speaks.

Accepting this power of interpretation as the dominant characteristic of modern poetry, I shall endeavour to indicate the methods in which it is respectively manifested when the poet interprets action, when he interprets nature, and when he interprets states of mind, individual or collective.

The forms of poetry—poetry including all creative literature whether in prose or verse—in which the interpretation of action is most successfully achieved are beyond question the drama—or more correctly dramatic compositions—and prose fiction. Both of these have become separate branches of the art of poetry, in the sense that they can be properly styled arts—and are so styled by competent authorities—the Drama and Fiction. The reason for this separation is not far to seek. When once thought has become dominant in poetry the representation of human action has tended to become of less importance in poetry strictly so called. As an element of poetry it has ceased to hold the pre-eminent position which it holds, for example, in Aristotle's account, and in Lessing's, and in Arnold's original account based upon his study of the Greek models.

On the other hand, the materials suitable for reproduction in the poetic presentation of action have largely increased in volume. Consequently the drama, separated from poetry, has become a composite art, a special art with special powers in which the new appliances, placed by science at the disposal of the modern stage-manager, can be suitably and fully employed. And so the old identity which existed in the Hellenic era, and which the French classical poets of the seventeenth century sought to recover, has been finally lost.

Similarly, Fiction as a separate art has many advantages, in respect of the delineation of human action, which poetry does not possess. In the use of the common medium, language, the novelist is unfettered by the restraints of metre; and in respect of structure, he is almost absolutely free. Consequently certain aspects of human action, and of human thought, which are unsuitable for poetry, can be treated without artistic impropriety in fiction; while there are others which can be treated more fully and more effectively.

As each of these specialised forms of poetry will be considered in a separate chapter, I shall confine myself for the present to an account of that method which is common to all forms of poetry in which the interpretation of action is a prominent element. Among them, of course, is included Epic and the lesser narrative poetry. Such poetry is not intended for stage representation, and it admits, therefore, of description and reflection; it possesses the artistic qualities associated with a precise and musical medium, verse or modulated language; on the other hand, action is its special object of imitation, and it is in its treatment of this aspect of life that it specially manifests its power of interpretation. In this poetry, as in the drama and the novel—in all poetry where action is the basis of the interpretation of life—the plot is the supreme element. The plot is to the poet what the 'composition' of the design is to the artist. It is the 'handling' of the subject, its treatment in the broadest sense. By his plot the poet defines the scope of his conception, and presents the ideas to which he wishes to give an artistic form in bold outline.

For the dramatist, and for the narrative poet in a less degree, the selection of certain characters and of certain incidents, the assignment of the parts which these characters are to severally play, and the arrangement of the incidents in due relation to each other, and to the characters, is the first and most significant operation. In this operation he is guided by the principles of art which limit both the objects and the method of poetic imitation. The objects of poetry are limited, for the poet must not reproduce all actions or every character, but only such as, when reproduced, are capable of being invested with a certain moral quality, and a certain artistic value. Its method is as precisely idealistic as that of Painting or Sculpture. The mass of materials thus selected must be endowed with form. Expression must be given to them by combining them in a plot, or scheme of action, which groups them under one or more main ideas. So too, with each individual action and character ; the characters must be 'typical,' the incidents must be 'probable.' Throughout this operation the poet interprets. He interprets the isolated actions of real persons, as we see them in real life, by exhibiting such actions in relation to general principles of human action ; and he interprets the individual man and woman of every day by exhibiting the classes, or types, to which they severally belong, and tracing the motives by which each class, as a class, is distinguished.

By his plot, therefore, the poet gives his broadest and most powerful interpretation of the facts of human life. Here, as the interpreter of life, it is his business to exhibit the working of the central passions of humanity, to present in sharp contrast the several effects of love and hate, honesty and fraud, licence and restraint ; to illustrate the humiliating dependence of man on matter, the uncertainty which characterises the possession of material endowments, physical power, rank and wealth ; the interdependence of man and man, the sudden dissolutions of human relationships by death.   All these he must exhibit by effective contrast.   But, in order to present the true significance of human life, he must show that man has an existence apart from these circumstances and relationships.   That by virtue of this existence he is independent of circumstances.   For this purpose he must so combine his characters and incidents as to exhibit the underlying control of a supreme intelligence, manifested in the working of physical and moral laws.   He must reconcile the prevalence of accident with the existence of design, and satisfy the inherent sense of justice, which is founded upon a belief in the existence of this supreme intelligence. In short, he must harmonise the facts of life with the moral sense.

The great problem of human life is the existence of evil.   And, therefore, one of the great objects of the poet's interpretation of life by plot, or interwoven action, is to exhibit a relationship between apparently undeserved calamity and some principle which is based upon natural or divine law, or on both.   For this purpose the Attic Tragedians employed the doctrine of Nemesis, or hereditary curse.   Regarded as a retribution for sin, Nemesis afforded a religious motive, and as such it could be suitably used when the drama was a religious institution. Of similar import is the Christian principle of duty, or submission to the will of God, associated with the belief in the immortality of the soul and the doctrine of future rewards and punishments. It is by reference to this principle that both the existence of the principle of evil and the fall of man are explained by Milton in *Paradise Lost.* In the law of heredity we have the scientific rendering of the Greek doctrine of Nemesis. And as such it has been used by 'George Eliot,' who has given us pictures of human life in which the law of heredity is exhibited both in the narrow sense of the transmission of physical and mental qualities from parent to child, and in the wider sense, in which the men and women of the present are regarded as already conditioned by the men and women of the past, and as themselves conditioning the men and women of the future. The interpretation which is here offered is no explanation, but the confession of the materialist that the attempt to interpret life without the recognition of a spiritual factor is impossible.

> ' Say we fail !
> We feed the high tradition of the world,
> And leave our spirit in our children's breasts.' [1]

Another determining principle of human life is the law of sexual attraction ; the 'old, old story,' which in the novelist's plot determines the fortunes of man and woman in the springtime of their existence. To exhibit this force in conflict with circumstances, or with the declared hostility of kinsfolk, to illustrate the text,

> ' The course of true love never did run smooth,'

is the common task of the English novelist ; but the same motive in the hands of Shakespeare has given

---

[1] *Spanish Gypsy.*

occasion for the masterpieces of *Romeo and Juliet* and *Othello.*

Moreover, this force, if it be abused or misused, becomes a fertile source of disaster. It causes constant complications in the normal human relationships, and even ventures to dispute the authority of reason.

Or, it may be the purpose of the poet to illustrate by his imagined characters truths and principles of less universal application. Such as the principle of *The Idylls of the King*—the doctrine of kingly responsibility.

> 'The king must guard
> That which he rules, and is but as the hind
> To whom a space of land is given to plow ;
> Who may not wander from the allotted field
> Before his work be done.'

Or that of *The Ring and the Book*—the insufficiency of human knowledge.

> 'This lesson, that our human speech is nought,
> Our human testimony false, our fame
> And human estimation words and wind.'

In the plot the poet deals with life in the mass : he also interprets it in detail.

Here it may be useful to refer for a moment to the distinction which Aristotle draws between the two typical poetic natures. 'Poetry,' he says, 'is an art which requires a man of genius or an enthusiast ; for, of these two classes, the former readily receive impressions, the latter are easily carried out of themselves.' [1] The poet, he has remarked, must realise what he portrays. This realisation may be the result of actual experience.

---

[1] *Poetics*, 1455ᵃ [reading ἐκστατικόι].

But as actual experience is necessarily limited, the poetic gifts are generally found in men who can realise what they portray without actually experiencing it. And so we get two natures which go to form poets— the sensitive (εὐφυὴς, εὔπλαστος), and the self-abandoning (μανικὸς, ἐκστατικός).

It is difficult to apply the distinction to individual poets, and with the increasing complexity of modern thought, the poetic nature tends to include both elements. If, however, we identify with the sensitive nature, the poet who alternately startles and delights us by attaching deeper meanings and fresh analogies to the common facts of life, and the common processes of nature, we cannot fail to recognise that it is on this side that poetry has especially developed in the present century. Such poets are, in the words of Joubert,[1] 'spirits who maintain that to see and exhibit things in beauty is to see and show things as in their essence they really are, and not as they exist for the careless, who do not look beyond the outside.'

This development is especially apparent in the treatment of nature in modern poetry. It is not only that descriptions of scenery and of the processes of nature occupy more space, as is the case to a conspicuous degree in the writings of Wordsworth and his school ; but the contemporary poet has learnt to approach Nature with a different object. If I may so express myself, whereas Sophocles and Shakespeare and Wordsworth interpret Nature, these contemporary poets first interrogate and then interpret.

Let me make my meaning plain. A wider scope was

[1] Quoted by Matthew Arnold in his *Essay on Joubert*.

given to the poetic interpretation of Nature, as well as
to that of human action, by the substitution of Christianity for the religious beliefs and philosophic systems
of the ancient world.   With the growth of Christianity
an earnest desire to transcend the sensuous—the seen
and perishable—and pass into the region of the spiritual
—the unseen and eternal—became part of the life not
merely of the learned but of the masses of mankind.
This wider scope of thought is characteristic of all
modern as compared with ancient poetry; and its
presence is unmistakably apparent in the poetry of the
Elizabethan age.   But the interrogation of nature has
been undertaken in response to the analytic tendency in
the thought of the Victorian age, and such treatment has
been made possible by the wide and easy diffusion of
knowledge, which has accompanied the discoveries of
science and their application to the wants of men.

To take examples.

In the first place there is no trace of this interrogation
of Nature in passages in which processes of Nature are
used simply to illustrate the life of man.   Such a passage
as this :

> 'This is the state of man : to-day he puts forth
> The tender leaves of hopes ; to-morrow blossoms,
> And bears his blushing honours thick upon him ;
> The third day comes a frost, a killing frost ;
> And, when he thinks, good easy man, full surely
> His greatness is a-ripening, nips his root,
> And then he falls, as I do.' [1]

Nor again, where the poet reproduces a feeling, or
state of mind, which arises in the presence of nature,

[1] *Henry VIII.*, Act iii. scene 2.

and exhibits the resemblance between this feeling and some phase of human thought or action.

> ' A day in April never came so sweet,
>   To show how costly summer was at hand,
>   As this fore-spurrer comes before his lord.' [1]

Nor is it present in merely descriptive passages. Such as,

> ' The moon shines bright : in such a night as this,
>   When the sweet wind did gently kiss the trees
>   And they did make no noise. . . .' [2]

Or,

> ' It was the lark, the herald of the morn,
>   No nightingale : look, love, what envious streaks
>   Do lace the severing clouds in yonder east ;
>   Night's candles are burnt out, and jocund day
>   Stands tiptoe on the misty mountain tops.' [3]

All these passages are interpretative of nature, but they are interpretative by virtue of the method of poetry. That is to say, the poet paints the scene not only by describing its external aspects, but by also describing the feelings which it produces in the mind of the spectator. But there is here no interrogation of nature ; nor is there any interpretation of nature in the sense which is characteristic of modern poetry, in the sense in which nature is interpreted in Wordsworth, and more rarely in Shakespeare. What the modern poet especially aims at, in endeavouring to satisfy the aspirations introduced into the common thought of men by Christianity, is to trace the working of a Supreme Intelligence, to point out how

---

[1] *Merchant of Venice*, Act ii. scene 9.   [2] *Ib.*, Act v. scene 1.
[3] *Romeo and Juliet*, Act iii. scene 5.

the beauty which appears on the face of nature is nothing less than the expression which has been given by this divine intelligence.   Shakespeare interprets nature in this sense when he says :

> ' Look how the floor of heaven
> Is thick inlaid with patines of bright gold.
> There's not the smallest orb which thou behold'st,
> But in his motion like an angel sings,
> Still quiring to the young-eyed cherubims :
> *Such harmony is in immortal souls ;*
> But whilst this muddy vesture of decay
> Doth grossly close it in, we cannot hear it.' [1]

Here the 'mind's excursive power,' as Wordsworth calls it, is satisfied ; and we pass beyond the sensuous into the spiritual world.   And Wordsworth is constantly occupied with an interpretation of nature in this sense. His attitude is that of his own child, listening to the murmur of the sea in ' a smooth-lipped shell.'

> ' I have seen
> A curious child, who dwelt upon a tract
> Of inland ground, applying to his ear
> The convolutions of a smooth-lipped shell ;
> To which, in silence hushed, his very soul
> Listened intensely ; and his countenance soon
> Brightened with joy ; for murmurings from within
> Were heard, sonorous cadences ! whereby
> To his belief, the monitor expressed
> Mysterious union with its native sea.
> Even such a shell the universe itself
> Is to the ear of faith ; and there are times,
> I doubt not, when to you it doth impart

---

[1] *Merchant of Venice*, Act v. sc. i.

Authentic tidings of invisible things ;
Of ebb and flow, and ever-during power ;
And central peace, subsisting at the heart
Of endless agitation.' [1]

But I have said that contemporary poets in their treatment of nature are touched by the analytic tendency of the age, and first interrogate and then interpret. Their attitude is no longer that of Wordsworth's child, passive and recipient ; it is active and inquiring. And for the purpose of illustrating this distinction I will add to the lines of Shakespeare which I have placed above, two passages taken respectively from Matthew Arnold and Browning, in which the same subject, the message of the stars, is treated.

' From the intense, clear, star-sown vault of heaven,
Over the lit sea's unquiet way,
In the rustling night-air came the answer :
" Would'st thou *be* as these are ? *Live* as they.

" Unaffrighted by the silence round them,
Undistracted by the sights they see,
These demand not that the things without them
Yield them love, amusement, sympathy.

" And with joy the stars perform their shining,
And the sea its long moon-silver'd roll ;
For self-poised they live, nor pine with noting
All the fever of some differing soul.

" Bounded by themselves and unregardful
In what state God's other works may be,
In their own tasks all their powers pouring,
These attain the mighty life you see." ' [2]

[1] *The Excursion*, Book IV.   [2] *Self-Dependence*.

To this argument Browning answers :—

> 'The stars, each orb
> Thou standest rapt beneath, proposes one :
> Do not they live their life, and please themselves,
> And so please thee ?   What more is requisite ?
> Make thou this answer : " If indeed no mage
> Opened my eyes and worked a miracle,
> Then let the stars thank me who apprehend
> That such an one is white, such other blue !
> But for my apprehension, both were blank . . .
> Cannot I close my eyes and bid my brain
> Make whites and blues, conceive without star's help
> New qualities of colour ? . . ."
> My mage for me !
> I never saw him : if he never was,
> I am the arbitrator.' [1]

But it is not only in this more earnest treatment of
nature that the poet responds to the quickened intellectual life of the age : he responds to it by an enlarged
and detailed consideration of psychological phenomena.
Man has his mental 'new worlds' revealed by the discoveries of science, as much as his physical 'new worlds'
revealed by the explorer and the coloniser.   The poet
of to-day is free to develop the poetic resources of these
new worlds of thought and sensation.   He has to reveal
the moral and spiritual aspects of our increased knowledge of the physical constitution both of man and of
nature, of organic and of inorganic matter.   He will
show how such laws as the conservation of energy, the
survival of the fittest, and the law of heredity, contain
a clearer and more exact manifestation of the working

[1] *Ferishtah Fancies*, p. 136.

of the Spiritual Principle in the physical world. He will indicate the new relationships in which man is placed towards God and towards his fellow-men by this clearer manifestation. He will show how the scope of human thought has been enlarged by the discoveries of mental science, and give expression to the clearer and more defined aspirations of man for communion with the unseen world and the spiritual principle, by which these discoveries have been accompanied.

In speaking of this aspect of the interpretation of life by poetry it is impossible to omit a reference to the work of Robert Browning. He is the one poet who has dealt fully and impartially with the spiritual difficulties of his contemporaries.

> ' Dost thou blame
> A soul that strives but to see plain, speak true,
> Truth at all hazards ?   Oh, this false for real,
> This emptiness which feigns solidity,—
> Ever some grey that's white and dun that's black,—
> When shall we rest upon the thing itself,
> Not on its semblance ?—Soul—too weak, forsooth,
> To cope with fact,—wants fiction everywhere !
> Mine tires of falsehood : truth at any cost !' [1]

In him the power of the man and the power of the moment are united : and, by approaching the solution of spiritual problems in an age when spiritual problems are all important, he perhaps more than any other poet embodies the spirit of the Victorian era. Broadly put, his interpretation of the new facts which have become incorporated into the life of man, is an endeavour to harmonise the teaching of science with the beliefs of

[1] Ib.

Christianity, in an All-powerful God, in free-will, and in the immortality of the soul. Such beliefs he felt to be ennobling and necessary, and he saw that no material advance would compensate for the spiritual discomfiture in which man would be involved, if he were deprived of them. At the same time he was prepared to face the truth *at any cost*. In his reconciliation he relies in the main on two doctrines—the relativity of knowledge, and the probationary character of man's life on earth. By the former he explains the impossibility of attaining exact knowledge in the sphere of morals and religious belief; by the latter, the existence of evil in a world which is governed by a Being who is both all-powerful and all-wise. He admits the impossibility of any final expression of knowledge, since the second half of the equation of truth (to borrow a phrase from George Henry Lewes) varies with the first, the form of the affirmation varies with the nature of the individual who affirms. But this variation does not, with him, render knowledge useless. On the contrary it explains apparent inconsistencies, and adds a greater dignity to religious beliefs, which epitomise the experience of the race. It is upon the limitations of the individual intelligence that he bases his recognition of a divine judgment, transcending human reason, and justifying the appeal of religion to faith. At the same time, while asserting that evil leads to good, he frankly admits that the ' how and why' of its existence will not be known until the race has far advanced in its development, or indeed, until the soul has reached the spirit world. And so he asks,

' What were life
Did soul stand still therein, forego her strife

> Through the ambiguous Present to the goal
> Of some all-reconciling Future ? ' [1]

And he speaks for his generation, when he says,

> ' The sum of all is : Yes, my doubt is great,
> My faith's still greater, then my faith's enough.' [2]

It remains to consider how poetry interprets states of mind individual or collective. It is in this aspect of the interpretation of life that the self-abandoning nature is prominent. The special power of the poet, thus constituted, is well described by Emerson.

' It is a secret which every intellectual man quickly learns, that, beyond the energy of his possessed and conscious intellect he is capable of a new energy (as of an intellect doubled on itself), by abandonment to the nature of things ; that, besides his privacy of power as an individual man, there is a great public power on which he can draw, by unlocking, at all risks, his human doors, and suffering the etherial tides to roll and circulate through him : then he is caught up into the life of the universe, his speech is thunder, his thought is law, and his words are as universally intelligible as the plants and animals. The poet knows that he speaks adequately, then, only when he speaks somewhat wildly, or " with the flower of his mind " ; not with the intellect, used as an organ, but with the intellect released from all service, and suffered to take its direction from its celestial life ; or, as the ancients were wont to express themselves, not with intellect alone, but with the intellect inebriated with nectar.' [3]

As a great elegiac poet, Matthew Arnold is the clearest exponent of the subjective aspect of the religious conflict of the Victorian era. He has helped the thinkers

[1] *Gerard de Lairesse.*　　　　[2] *Men and Women.*
[3] *Essay on ' The Poet.'*

of his generation to find an utterance for their sadness ;
he has interpreted their feelings. This sadness, this
conflict, he has said, is natural, it is not beyond explanation ; and he has, in his later poems, expressed his hope
of an ultimate reconciliation between doubt and belief.
No one has laid bare the 'malady of the century' with
keener insight than he :

> '. . . this strange disease of modern life,
>   With its sick hurry, its divided aims,
>   Its heads o'ertaxed, its palsied hearts . . .' [1]

Nor has any better explained the recoil to medi-
ævalism, which has resulted from it.

> 'Oh, hide me in your gloom profound,
>   Ye solemn seats of holy pain !
> Take me, cowl'd forms, and fence me round,
>   Till I possess my soul again ;
> Till free my thoughts before me roll,
>   Not chafed by hourly false control !' [2]

Or, the increased appreciation of the 'plan of
nature.'

> 'Calm soul of things ! make it mine
>   To feel, amid the city's jar,
> That there abides a peace of thine,
>   Man did not make, and cannot mar.
>
> The will to neither strive nor cry,
>   The power to feel with others give !
> Calm, calm me more ! nor let me die
>   Before I have begun to live.' [3]

[1] *Scholar Gypsy.*   [2] *Stanzas from the Grande Chartreuse.*
[3] *Lines written in Kensington Gardens.*

Or, the growing belief in the restoration of faith.

> ' The world's great order dawns in sheen,
>   After long darkness rude,
>   Divinelier imaged, clearer seen,
>   With happier zeal pursued.' [1]

In contrast to Matthew Arnold and Browning, Tennyson has interpreted the life of the age on the side of action. From the first he had identified himself with the life of the nation, and as years advanced he came to speak with increasing authority. In certain splendid utterances which mark his later years, ' his word,' as Emerson says, ' has become law,' his voice has become the voice of England. Relying upon this ' public power,' he has expressed the widely diffused distrust of that aspect of the dominant political movement which is characterised by the term ' democracy.'

' Charm us, Orator, till the Lion look no larger than the Cat,

Till the Cat thro' that mirage of over-heated language loom
Larger than the Lion,—Demos end in working its own
    doom.

Russia bursts our Indian barrier, shall we fight her? shall
    we yield?
Pause before you sound the trumpet, hear the voices from
    the field.

Those three hundred millions under one Imperial sceptre
    now,
Shall we hold them? Shall we loose them? Take the
    suffrage of the plow.

[1] *Obermann Once More.*

Nay, but these would feel and follow truth, if only you and
you,
Rivals of realm-ruining party, when you speak were wholly
true.' [1]

Even stronger is the expression of the recoil against
materialism which he gives in *Despair*.

' Oh, we poor orphans of nothing—alone on that lonely shore—
Born of the brainless nature who knew not that which she
bore !
Trusting no longer that earthly flower would be heavenly
fruit—
Come from the brute, poor souls—no souls—and to die with
the brute.'

With equal precision and authority he has interpreted
the national aspirations which have grown with the
extension of the Anglo-Saxon race. Persistently and
emphatically, he expresses the belief that the supremacy
of that race depends upon its morality.

' Handful of men as we were, we were English in heart and
limb,
Strong with the strength of the race, *to command, to obey, to
endure*.' [2]

He has reflected these aspirations in their more defined
form of Imperial Unity.

' The loyal to their Crown
Are loyal to their own far sons, who love
Our ocean-empire with her boundless homes
For ever-broadening England, and her throne

[1] *Locksley Hall—Sixty Years After.*   [2] *Defence of Lucknow.*

In our vast Orient, and one isle, one isle
That knows not her own greatness : if she knows
And dreads it we are fall'n.' [1]

I have suggested that poetry has developed in the direction of thought, and that poetry, strictly so called, owing to the separation of the Drama and the growth of Fiction, has tended to exercise its interpretative power less by means of action and character and more by the study of nature and psychological phenomena. More than one Victorian poet might be cited in support of this contention, but one name is conspicuous. Mr. Swinburne interprets the spirit of freedom in its fullest developments. It is sufficient to say that in so doing he has treated the ideas associated with Republican principles, free-thought, and scientific ethics, with the power and charm of a great master of song. Both his own lyric genius, and the nature of the subjects which he has chosen for his more serious poetic effort, make his work a supreme example of the power of poetry to interpret even the most subtle and elusive aspects of modern thought.

He represents Christianity from the materialist standpoint as a light that has failed.

' Christian, what of the night ?—
I cannot tell ; I am blind.
I halt and hearken behind
If haply the hours will go back
And return to the dear dead light,
To the watch-fires and stars that of old
Shone where the sky now is black,
Glowed where the earth now is cold.' [2]

[1] Dedication of the *Idylls of the King*.   [2] *A Watch in the Night*.

As an exponent of the 'religion of humanity' he presents a conception of duty in 'The Pilgrims,' which is absolutely free from any trace of utility, where there is no gain either in this world or the next, except such as arises from the consciousness of doing right; a conception, in short, wholly spiritual. In answer to the question, 'Who is your lady of love, Oh ye that pass singing?' these Pilgrims, the representatives of the new faith, reply that it is a Queen, who can give them no immediate nor material reward. Then follow other questions and answers.

> '—And ye shall die before your thrones be won?
> —Yea, and the changed world and the liberal sun
> Shall move and shine without us, and we lie
>   Dead; but if she too move on earth and live,
> But if the old world with all the old irons rent
> Laugh and give thanks, shall we not be content?
>   Nay, we shall rather live, we shall not die,
>   Life being so little and death so good to give.'

And life is for such what it was for Heine—the 'liberation war of humanity.'

> ' A little time that we may fill
>   Or with such good works or such ill
>   As loose the bonds or make them strong
>   Wherein all manhood suffers wrong.
> By rose-hung river and light-foot rill
>   There are who rest not; who think long
>   Till they discern as from a hill
>   At the sun's hour of morning-song,
> Known of souls only, and those souls free,
> The sacred spaces of the sea.' [1]

[1] Prelude to *Songs before Sunrise.*

All these are delicate records of states of mind which represent ideas so ethereal as almost to elude the attempt to express them in words. I cite these passages, therefore, not so much as examples of Mr. Swinburne's poetry, but rather as examples of the high degree of development to which poetry has attained as the interpreter of thought.

CHAPTER X

THE DRAMA AS A COMPOSITE ART

IF in literature the internal element has become all-important, in the drama the external element has acquired an equal significance. That which the drama has, and literature has not, is stage representation; and it is this—the representation of the real by the real—which makes the drama a separate art. But the representation of the real by the real is not identical with the reality of ordinary life. It is necessary to have this fact clearly before us at the outset; the fact that actuality, not reality, reality heightened and intensified by concentration, something that is not less, but more than reality, is the essence of the drama.

It is a selected specimen of life rather than life itself which is brought upon the stage : the play of mind is more strenuous, the colour is brighter, the sound is clearer and more musical, the action is more decisive, the characters are types, not individuals, the atmosphere in which they move is more electric. The drama is more real than life. If this be allowed, the difficulty of accepting the realism of the stage, when we refuse to recognise the realism of painting and poetry, vanishes.

But how can this be ? A moment's consideration will

show that it is not a paradox, but a truth. Life, the sense of life, is measured by sensation, not by existence. Sensation depends upon two factors—external stimuli and the individual mind. If a combination of external stimuli can be so arranged as to produce an effect upon the mind, more powerful and more varied than any effect produced in the ordinary experience of everyday life, then the result achieved is an increase of sensation, and this increased sensation brings with it an increased sense of life. I deal with averages, not with exceptional cases. There are moments of supreme intensity in the life of every one, when the sense of life is realised in a supreme degree. I omit these from the comparison. As thus limited, the proposition that the sense of life, which the drama produces in the mind of the spectator, is greater than that which he ordinarily experiences, will commend itself to every observer.

Even in the Greek tragedy Aristotle notices the power to produce sensation as a distinctive merit. 'Tragedy,'[1] he says, 'has all that Epic has, and in addition a very considerable element of power in music and scenic accessories ; and it is music which gives the greatest vividness to the combination of pleasurable emotions produced by Tragedy.' And the Greek drama was immeasurably inferior in actuality to the modern drama.

The history of the drama begins with sensation, and it seems probable that it will end in sensation. The powerful but vague emotion aroused by music and the dance was expressed in the rustic ballad dance performed in honour of Dionysus ; and the dithyramb was the

[1] *Poetics*, 1462ᵃ.

progenitor alike of tragedy and comedy. The ebb and
flow of human passion was present in this manifestation
of elementary impulses ; desire and satiety, joy and
sorrow, activity and rest followed in natural alternation,
and each element was appropriated and developed by one
of the two poetic temperaments, the grave and brooding,
and the gay and sensuous. 'What divided poetry,'
Aristotle says, 'was the divergences of individual character.
For while the graver poets imitated noble actions and
the actions of noble persons, the lighter took those of
worthless persons for their subjects, commencing with
lampoons, as the former had commenced with hymns
and encomia.' [1]

Thus the vintage song and village revel both developed
into musical performances, rendered by a trained chorus,
who united in rhythmic movements which expressed the
dominant feeling of the words they sung. To the lyric
element, introduced by the choral odes, was added an
epic element, the 'episodes,' or parenthetic passages, recited between the choral performances. The rhapsodist
became first the equal, and afterwards the superior of the
coryphæus. The 'answerer' became the actor, and the
episodes the drama. But before this change, the dramatic
poet had, in his desire to provide his characters with a
diction approaching most nearly to that of common
speech, substituted the quick iambics of satire for the
leisured hexameters of Epic. And so tragedy, where the
seriousness of true poetry was preserved, was for Aristotle the highest and most developed form of 'poetry.'
It had gradually united in itself the best elements
of Lyric, Epic, and satire ; it retained within due

[1] Ib., 1448[b].

limits the services of instrumental music, of rhythmic motion and gesture, and it had added those of stage representation.

And in the modern drama a like process of growth and selection may be observed. In its advance towards specialisation it has tended to divest itself of certain elements of poetry and to extend others; and in addition it has allied itself in an increasing degree with the 'arts of the eye.' The differences between the Greek and the modern drama are significant, for an examination of these differences indicates in the clearest manner the special objects which the dramatic artist and the actor unitedly seek to achieve to-day.

The structure of the Greek drama in its representative form of tragedy is described by Aristotle.[1] 'The parts in the sense of separate divisions,' he says, 'are as follows : Prologue, episode, exodus, and chorus, which last includes odes rendered in procession or otherwise.' That is to say, the tragedy in its perfect form consisted of a prologue, a choral ode marking the entry of the chorus, the actual drama presented in episodes divided by choral interludes, and the choral ode which marked the withdrawal of the chorus and the completion of the performance. From another point of view, he says :[2] 'Every tragedy consists of two parts, development ($\delta\acute{\epsilon}\sigma\iota\varsigma$) and solution ($\lambda\acute{\upsilon}\sigma\iota\varsigma$). The incidents outside the main action, and often some of those included in it, form the development ; what remains is the solution.' It appears, therefore, that the progress of the action in the Greek tragedy, as represented here, does not differ materially from that of the five-act play. The relation of the two may be shown by

[1] Ib., 1452b.   [2] Ib., 1455b.

comparing the curve of an ellipse with that of a parabola.

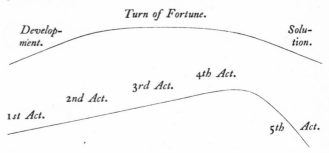

Turn of Fortune.

Develop-ment.

Solu-tion.

4th Act.

3rd Act.

2nd Act.

1st Act.

5th Act.

But the Greek tragedy was rigidly limited in respect of the number of actors, the structure and character of the plot, and in stage representation.

The number of actors was confined to three, or at most four, aided, however, by the 'messenger' and the leader of the chorus.

The plot, which was the 'soul' of the drama, was confined both in construction and in subject.   Unity of plot restrained the presentation of supplementary action by episodes.   Both the religious element, and the relation-ship of the drama to the State, restricted the poet in the choice of subjects.   Comedy was more free in this respect than tragedy.   There, as Aristotle says,[1] the difference between the method of poetry and that of history was earlier recognised, and the comic poet discarded both traditional plots and traditional names.

But in respect of tragedy he tells us that the scope of subject was recognised as practically limited to the

[1] Ib., 1451ᵇ.

presentation of a few well-known and familiar myths.
'For,' he adds,[1] 'it was chance, not art, which led the
poets in their search to find the required situation in the
myths. They are compelled, therefore, to have recourse
to those heroic houses whose history is marked by tragic
events.'

But most of all the Greek drama was limited in respect
of stage representation. The vast theatre open to the
sky, the enormous audience, the masks and buskins worn
by the actors, all united to exclude any play of feature,
any pure elocution, or any spontaneous movement or
gesture. The conditions under which the Greek drama
was presented on the stage, and the limitations which
these conditions involved, are excellently portrayed by
Professor Lewis Campbell. In commenting upon Aristotle's statement that the pursuit of Hector, as described
by Homer, would appear absurd if represented on the
stage, he writes : [2]

'One can readily understand how the notion of Achilles
pursuing Hector on the stage suggested itself to Aristotle as
the height of absurdity. The grouped figures thus [*i.e.*
raised by the "buskins"], as it were, brought nearer to the
eye (in the absence of magnifying lenses), must often have
seemed as still as in a *tableau vivant*—the "dumb personages" (κῶφα πρόσωπα) and other supernumeraries adding to
the effect. The actor was a sort of speaking statue, or at
least one who in motion, voice, and gesture resembled Aristotle's magnanimous man, whose gait is slow and his voice
monotonous and deep. The whole scene bore a majestic
resemblance to the marble reliefs with which in later times
the stage was adorned, much as the Panathenaic procession
was itself reflected in the Parthenon frieze. It by no means

[1] Ib., 1454[a].   [2] *Greek Tragedy*, pp. 90-91.

follows that the effect produced was mechanical or unnatural. It should rather be said that the expression of sustained passion under those conditions required an intensity of realisation, such as few even of the greatest actors have ever displayed. To maintain with dignified pose and gesture the character which the poet intended, and which the maker of the mask had stamped in statuesque nobility upon the face; to make felt by every one of the 30,000 spectators the significance of every cadence, and above all, through the slow and measured rhythm, which alone could be followed by such a multitude, to carry home the warmth and vehemence of strong emotion, must have required powers and accomplishments of no mean order.'

The differences in the conditions under which the modern drama is presented on the stage are too obvious to need description. It is sufficient merely to point out that the comparative smallness of the theatre makes play of feature, significance of gesture, and intonation and vibration of voice, possible for the actor, and that scenic accessories are becoming more perfect every day.

In structure the modern drama, as we have seen, follows the broad lines of the Greek tragedy. But the plot has been developed, and the function of the actor has grown out of all knowledge. The conception of plot in general has changed with the growth of poetry. What this conception is in its wider aspects, will have appeared from the account of 'poetic justice' already given.[1] As an element of drama, it is well described[2] by Mr. R. G. Moulton, in his study of Shakespeare.

'If plot be understood as the extension of design to the sphere of human life, threads of experience being woven into

[1] Chapter iv.   [2] *Shakespeare as a Dramatic Artist*, pp. 310, 311.

a symmetrical pattern as truly as vari-coloured threads of
wool are woven into a piece of woolwork, then the conception of it will come out in its true dignity.   What else is such
reduction to order than the meeting-point of science and art ?
Science is engaged in tracing rhythmic movements in the
beautiful confusion of the heavenly bodies, or reducing the
bewildering variety of external nature to regular species and
nice gradations of life.   Similarly, art continues the work of
creation in calling ideal order out of the chaos of things as
they are.   And so the tangle of life, with its jumble of con-
flicting aspirations, its crossing and twisting of contrary
motives, its struggle and partnership of the whole human
race, in which no two individuals are perfectly alike, and no
one is wholly independent of the rest—this has gradually in
the course of ages been laboriously traced by the scientific
historian into some such harmonious plan as evolution.   But
he finds himself long ago anticipated by the dramatic artist,
who has touched crime and seen it link itself with Nemesis,
who has transformed passion into pathos, who has received
the shapeless facts of reality and returned them as an ordered
economy of design.   This application of form to human life
is Plot ; and Shakespeare has no higher task to accomplish
than in his revolutionising our ideas of plot, until the old
critical conceptions of it completely broke down when applied
to his dramas.'

   The increased power of the actor is due to the changed
conditions of stage representation.   The modern actor
does not merely recite the words of the poet with
appropriate movement and gesture ; he interprets and
creates.   The actor can, as George Stevens said to
Garrick, clear ' with a single look or a particular modu-
lation of the voice ' a difficulty which ' a long and
laboured paraphrase was insufficient to explain.'   He

invests the words he utters and the actions he portrays
with a new meaning, and surprises even the author
himself, as Lekain did Voltaire. He does not interpret
merely by play of feature and intonation of voice, he
adds something to the conception of the poet. This
something is in part the result of previous study of the
character he represents, and in part, as Talma said, the
yielding of himself 'to the spontaneous flashes of his
sensibility, and all the emotions which it voluntarily
produces in him.' Under the present conditions of the
drama, complete illusion in scenery, and historic accuracy
in dress and detail, are at once possible and necessary.
And thus the Shakespearian drama is more developed
to-day than it was in the seventeenth century. The
dramatic compositions which bear the name of Shakespeare are the same, but the drama, the actual presentation
of these poetic masterpieces on the stage by means of
actors and scenery, is more powerful and more beautiful.
In precisely this sense Sir Henry Irving pleads for 'as
perfect a stage representation of Shakespeare as modern
art can furnish.' He writes :

'Acting is an art as distinct as any other, and, if it be the
most fleeting, is also the most vivid. . . . Is it nothing that
while the spirit of the poet is preserved, his ideas are illustrated by scholarly detail, by harmonious pictures, by appropriate music, by all that appeals to the sense of beauty ? We
do not quarrel with the novelist when he describes the scene
in which his creations live and move. How many famous
passages in fiction can be quoted to show that a word-picture
adds infinite force or charms to the most dramatic episode
of human passion ! So, on the stage, the accessories which
are perfectly attuned to the story must greatly enhance its

fascination. I have heard that some people still hold that we should play Shakespeare very much as he was played in his own time. But is one art to stand still while others progress, or rather is the stage to repudiate all the aids of painting and music, to disdain the fruits of historical inquiry, to shun the archæologist and the antiquarian? Would my readers like to banish pictures from their books? I am not pleading for pageants. Acting, and acting only, can make a play successful; but let us acknowledge that, by the legitimate arts of the stage, history and poetry may be illuminated for the dullest understanding, and a new zest added to the pleasures of refined taste.' [1]

Even when the dramatic composition, the contribution of the poet, remains unchanged, the drama can advance. Here, then, we have a clear indication of the direction in which it is developing. It develops in the direction of actuality. Where the poet's contribution remains unchanged, the development appears in the improved methods of stage representation ; where new poetic matter is supplied, in addition to this, the dramatic composition exhibits developments which it shares with creative literature as such.

The advance of the drama, produced by the joint action of both these causes, can be grouped under four heads : (1) a wider range of subjects ; (2) the use of prose instead of verse ; (3) the increased contribution of the actor himself; and (4) the gradual approach to visual actuality in stage representation.

Of these developments, the first, the adoption of a wider range of subjects, is one which is especially manifest in the two special arts which have grown out of poetry, the drama and fiction. Both of these arts are peculiarly

[1] *Shakespeare on the Stage and in the Study.*

sensitive to two forces which are especially active at the present time—scientific research and democracy. And each of these forces has alike tended to produce an indiscriminate representation of all phases and forms of human life in creative literature and art. The general effect so produced is well illustrated by a comparison of the respective methods of photography and painting. In a photographic picture there is no selection and only a limited arrangement, the appearance of the moment, and not the idealised, or generalised, appearance of the person or landscape, is reproduced ; and this exact, inclusive, photographic treatment is precisely the treatment of life which marks the modern drama and modern fiction.

But in comparison with fiction, the drama is limited in its range of subjects by the fact which Aristotle states with his usual directness, when he says that Epic has a wider range than tragedy because 'the action is not before our eyes.' 'In tragedies,' he says,[1] 'there must be an element of marvel, but in Epic there is more scope for that which is the strongest instrument in producing the marvellous—the improbable ; because the action is not before our eyes.' And the example he gives is the pursuit of Hector as described by Homer ; it is a scene which would be absurd on the stage, but in the poem the absurdity is not noticed.

Even in the drama the test of poetic truth is not entirely the verdict of the senses and of the reason, but this, together with something else which Aristotle does not clearly distinguish, but which we distinguish as the verdict of the imagination. Nevertheless the perception

[1] *Poetics*, 1460ᵃ.

of this something else leads him to the general principle which is applicable to all poetic creation—'the poet should choose what is impossible but likely, in preference to what is possible but incredible.' Judged by the evidence of the senses, and of reason, the appearance of Cæsar's ghost in the tent of Brutus on the eve of Philippi, is an impossibility ; but the appearance of the dead to the living is an idea so familiar to the mind of man that the incident, when represented on the stage, produces no sense of incongruity in the spectator. The imagination decides that it is 'likely,' however much the reason may decide that it is 'impossible.' In fiction, and in all creative literature apart from dramatic compositions, the verdict of the imagination is infinitely more important than the verdict of the senses, because it is to this faculty of the mind that the appeal of art is directed. And this fact gives fiction an advantage over the drama. As a means of portraying human life in its entirety, human life which includes mental phenomena as well as action, fiction has this obvious advantage over the drama, that the action is not before our physical but before our mental vision.

In respect of the change of subject-matter which the modern drama exhibits as compared with the Elizabethan drama, it will be obvious to the least careful observer of modern stage-plays, that the broad issues of human life, which were brought before the Elizabethan Englishmen, are almost entirely forsaken by the modern playwright. He relies upon minute issues, some of which would have been too fine for the actual comprehension of the Elizabethan playgoers. Apart from plays which are descriptive, or informing, or merely humorous, the tendency of the serious drama sets towards the 'problem' play. In its extreme form the problem play lends itself to the treatment of the questions of marriage and heredity by Hendrik Ibsen : in any case it affords abundant evidence of the minuteness, of the temporary and even topical character, of the issues which provide a motive for a modern play. It is significant, too, that the practice of dramatising novels is becoming increasingly common. The precise appreciation of human motive, the exact and complete analysis of character, which mark the novel, are, *mutatis mutandis*, equally important in the stage play. This minute treatment is only possible in the case of subjects and characters which are commonplace, and, therefore, familiar to the audience either from conventional accounts or from the experience of real life. And the modern playwright uses the commonplace subjects almost to the exclusion of history and religion.

Another obvious gain in actuality is secured by the substitution of prose for verse ; for people do not speak in verse. Practical experience has shown that success is much more easily secured if prose be used instead of verse, as the medium of dramatic composition. Entire failure, or, at best, only partial success, has attended the attempt to place the dramatic works of the greatest contemporary poets upon the stage. At the same time the transition is especially easy for the English dramatist. In Shakespeare we have, apart from the use of prose in passages which are humorous or familiar, a frequent interchange between the two mediums. Scenes in verse alternate with scenes in prose, speeches in verse with speeches in prose, and sometimes a speech which is begun

in the one and finished in the other.[1] Nor is there any
loss of poetic power. Generally, prose is employed to
give expression to humorous or commonplace thoughts
and ideas. But this is not a universal rule. If Portia
rises to her greatest height by the smooth flow of the
' majestic English iambics,' in

> ' The quality of mercy is not strain'd,
>   It droppeth as the gentle rain from heaven
>   Upon the place beneath : it is twice blest ;
>   It blesseth him that gives and him that takes :
>   'Tis mightiest in the mightiest : it becomes
>   The throned monarch better than his crown ;
>   His sceptre shows the force of temporal power,
>   The attribute to awe and majesty,
>   Wherein doth sit the dread and fear of kings ;
>   But mercy is above this sceptred sway ;
>   It is enthroned in the heart of kings,
>   It is an attribute to God himself ;
>   And earthly power doth then show likest God's
>   When mercy seasons justice '—

Shylock is most powerful in the torrent of words in which
he pours out his concentrated hate.

' Hath not a Jew eyes ? Hath not a Jew hands, organs,
dimensions, senses, affections, passions ? Fed with the same
food, hurt with the same weapons, subject to the same diseases,
healed by the same means, warmed and cooled by the same
winter and summer, as a Christian is ? If you prick us, do we
not bleed ? If you tickle us, do we not laugh ? If you poison
us, do we not die ? And if you wrong us, shall we not revenge ?'

And in Shakespeare blank verse was in itself, as Addison
calls it, ' a due medium between rhyme and prose.'

[1] *e.g. Henry IV.,* Part I. Act iii. scene 3.

Again, while blank verse sinks into prose, the finest English prose rises into hexameters. Such hexameters are found in the Authorised Version :   He *poureth contempt upon princes and weakeneth the strength of the mighty,* and *God is gone up with a shout, the Lord with a sound of a trumpet.* And in this connection it is worthy of remembrance that Mr. Swinburne, in his contempt for the English forms of this metre, has called Clough's hexameters 'studies in graduated prose.'

A factor in the change has been undoubtedly the adoption of more ordinary and commonplace subjects—the fact that the dramatic composer, with rare exceptions, pitches his drama in the key of everyday life. But, however the change has come about, the tendency of the modern drama, both in respect of subject and of medium, is towards actuality.

But the advance of the drama is unquestionably greatest in respect of the increased power of the actor, and the improvement of scenic appliances.

Mr. William Archer, in a series of papers entitled *The Anatomy of Acting,* traverses Diderot's *paradoxe* that the great actor is the man who feels least ; the man who like Lekain retains so complete a mastery of himself, that he can push a jewel to the wings with his foot at the moment when the tragic interest is at its highest.[1] For this purpose Mr. Archer drew up a series of questions, which became known as 'The Actor's Catechism.' [2]   These questions were circulated among a number of actors and actresses, with a view of collecting

[1] Lekain (as Ninias) saved the jewel which had been dropped by accident on the stage.

[2] Mr. Archer's papers were published in *Longmans' Magazine.*

evidence on the question in dispute. The general result of the information contained in the answers received was to establish the fact, that to a very large degree the actor does really feel the emotions which he portrays ; that his tears are often real tears, and his laughter is often natural laughter. He sums up the result in the following sentence :

'Nature has so compounded us that the imagination of certain mental states tends to beget in us the physical conditions and symptoms appropriate to these states.'

And,

'The artist who avails himself of this tendency . . . follows the line of least resistance.'

As a practical principle he advances the proposition : 'Do not trust to inspiration, but use inspiration where it comes.'

The whole of the very interesting evidence upon which this result is based tends to show that the interpretation of the part of the actor, that is to say, that the personal contribution made by the actor, is of increasing importance. This contribution is partly the result of study off the stage, and partly the result of inspiration on the stage. The source of this latter element, the extemporary element we may call it, is that very sensibility the absence of which, according to Diderot, has characterised the greatest actors. Undoubtedly the field within which this extemporary element can be manifested is very limited. The actor is limited by the fact that he acts in conjunction with others, and that, therefore, any departure from the text of the dialogue, even an unexpected gesture, may disarrange the harmony secured by the rehearsals ; he is limited also by the physical conditions of the stage and scenic accessories. But subject to these limitations the use of this extemporary element is exceedingly valuable. Mr. Archer records many instances, taken from actual experience, which show that when an actor can incorporate natural sensation into his acting, he produces a marvellous and electrical effect upon the audience. From these instances I venture to select the following as most typical :

'Mr. Clayton relates an amusing, yet really valuable, instance of inspiration. Salome, in *Dandy Dick*, has just read from the *Times* the paragraph announcing the Dean's munificent offer of £1000 to the Minster Restoration Fund, "on condition that seven other donors come forward, each with the like sum." "And will they ?" cries Sheba eagerly ; whereupon the Dean, who has been standing with his back to the audience, turns with an unctuous yet sickly smile, and replies : "My darling, times are bad, but one never knows." This smile was an inspiration. For some time after the production of the play Mr. Clayton used to speak the line gravely and meditatively, without producing any effect. One evening the smile—a really admirable trait —came to his lips almost before he knew what he was doing. The audience rose to it immediately, and from that day forward the speech, thus accentuated, remained one of the most successful in the piece.'

Moreover, Mr. Archer's evidence serves to bring out a point which is interesting in itself, and which has a direct bearing upon the main question. This point is the value of 'experience' as part of the mental furnishing of the actor. It is the truth which Aristotle states in respect of the dramatic composer :

'Given the same natural ability, those who experience what they portray are most effective. He who is himself vexed with the storms of misfortune, or driven wild with rage, will give the most faithful representation of such experiences.'[1]

It would seem, then, that with rare exceptions it is not until the actor has himself been stirred by some experience of the deeper issues of human life, until he has himself felt the deepened consciousness which comes in the presence of a great disaster, when the true relationship of the self to the external world is suddenly revealed, that he can rise to the full height of his interpretative function. And what applies to the highest emotions displayed in the supreme moments of the tragedy, applies also in a lesser degree to all incidents into which emotion, painful or joyous, enters. The actor must have a fund of personal experience to draw upon, and a trained capacity for feeling and displaying emotion, before he can represent emotion upon the stage.

With respect to the development of the drama in stage representation, I assume that the most complete command of scenic accessories is an acknowledged merit ; and I propose, therefore, merely to suggest a principle which seems to fix the one and only limit which can be placed legitimately upon the stage-manager's advance towards absolute visual actuality.

The drama is an art. What the poet, the actor, and the stage-manager combine in producing is a work of art, and, therefore, must be beautiful. 'Whatever feelings,' says Victor Cousin,[2] 'art purposes to excite in us, they ought always to be restrained and governed

[1] *Poetics*, 1455ᵃ·   [2] *Du Vrai, du Beau, et du Bien*, p. 183.

by the feeling of beauty. If it produces only pity or terror beyond a certain limit, above all physical pity or terror, it revolts, it ceases to charm ; it misses its proper effect for an effect which is foreign to it and vulgar.'

But this principle limits the realism of the stage, not in the manner of representation, but in the choice of the subject which is to be represented. It places no restraint upon the realistic treatment of that which can be legitimately represented on the stage, but it wholly forbids the representation of subjects which cannot be invested with either physical or moral beauty. When Cousin says, 'If I believed that Iphigeneia was really on the point of being offered in sacrifice by her father twenty paces from me, I should leave the theatre shuddering with horror,' and proceeds to argue against illusion, he misses the point. The effect to which he appeals does not provide an argument against illusion, but against the presentation of scenes of horror upon the stage at all. If Iphigeneia is to be sacrificed upon the stage, she had better be sacrificed with a due regard to historical accuracy and natural propriety ; otherwise the effect would be merely ludicrous. But where in the drama the senses can be legitimately beguiled—that is to say, when a belief in the reality of what he sees and hears does not interfere with the spectator's sense of beauty— complete illusion is the natural and proper goal towards which the stage-manager's efforts are directed.

One word in conclusion. If this be so—that is to say, if the drama develops in the direction of actuality—the attempt to apply an exclusively literary test to the performance of the modern stage must be a mistake. Yet this is what is being done now by those alarmists who are for ever prophesying evil. Let us take heart. The Shakespearian drama has developed, though Shakespeare has added no word to the contribution which he made to that drama in the Elizabethan age. And though men of creative talent should devote their power more and more to poetry and prose fiction, and leave the writing of plays to the playwright, the drama may yet progress towards its goal, may yet become a more beautiful and a more perfect art.

CHAPTER XI

EACH year the returns of the booksellers and the reports of the librarians testify afresh to the predominance of the novel in the world of books; and this evidence is supported by the everyday experience of each one of us. But, although the popularity of the novel has become a matter of common knowledge, the reasons for the predominance of this form of literature are not so well understood. And therefore, in an attempt to explain what is certainly a striking characteristic of nineteenth-century literature, it is desirable to have before us some statement which will show more precisely in what this predominance consists. Such a statement is afforded by a passage in Sir Walter Besant's *Art of Fiction*, in which he focuses the diffused impressions of common experience and observation to a clear conception.

'The modern novel,' he writes, 'converts abstract ideas into living models; it gives ideas, it strengthens faith, it preaches a higher morality than is seen in the actual world; it commands the emotions of pity, admiration, and terror; it creates and keeps alive the sense of sympathy; it is the universal teacher; it is the only book which the great mass of reading mankind ever do read; it is the only way in which people can learn what other men and women are like; it redeems their lives from dulness, puts thoughts, desires, knowledge, and even ambitions into their hearts; it teaches them to talk, and enriches their speech with epigrams, anecdotes, and illustrations. It is an unfailing source of delight to millions, happily not too critical. Why, out of all the books taken down from the shelves of the public libraries, four-fifths are novels, and of all those that are bought nine-tenths are novels. Compared with this tremendous engine of popular influence, what are all the other arts put together? Can we not alter the old maxim, and say with truth, Let him who pleases make the laws, if I may write the novels?'[1]

Without endorsing every expression in this panegyric we may take this much as established—that in the novel we have a great informing agency, a power which has already been used in the past, and which will be used in an increasing degree in the future, to affect human character for both good and evil. What is not yet determined is its literary value. Is it more than an informing agency? As a form of literature, has it attained to artistic merit? Or, failing this now, is it capable of such artistic development in the future as will win it a secure place in the circle of the Arts?

Sir Walter Besant has already made up his mind on the point, for he commences his address with the proposition, that 'Fiction is an Art in every way worthy to be called the sister and the equal of the arts of Painting, Sculpture, Music, and Poetry.' But there are many who do not share this confidence. They point out that the very circumstance which gives the novel its vogue— its adaptability to the needs of contemporary thought, its sensitiveness to the influence of Science and Democracy, the dominant forces of the nineteenth century—tends to prevent it from becoming amenable to the exclusive tests

---

[1] *Art of Fiction*, a lecture delivered at the Royal Institution, 1884.

of art. Its very popularity, in short, prevents it from assuming an artistic form, and thereby takes it out of the category of genuine poetic literature.

It is with a view of contributing to the solution of this question that I propose to discuss the nature and capacity of the novel as a form of literature. And in order to prevent any possible misconception I would declare without delay that in criticism I adopt the idealistic standpoint in its entirety : the standpoint, that is, of Plato and his modern disciple, Victor Cousin, that in literature thought is prior to form, and that excellence in art and literature is inseparably connected with the moral worth of the artist. Further, if I confine my inquiry to English novels, I would suggest that this limitation of the area of observation is not so injurious as it might seem at first sight. For the English novel has a special significance at the present time. In the first place, the growth of the English-speaking communities has made the English book-market the largest in the world ; and in the second, the English novel retains a moral purpose among its aims.

A review of the field of creative literature in the nineteenth century reveals two tendencies which have contributed to give the novel its present importance, and which promise to maintain or increase its importance in the future.

The first of these is the tendency of the modern stage to develop in the direction of actuality. The drama is, and always has been, a composite art ; but of the three elements which go to make up the effect produced by this composite art—literature, stage-presentation, and the actor's interpretation of his part by gesture and intonation —the first, the poet's contribution, has plainly declined in importance as compared with the two latter. This cause, and the increased vigour of other agencies for the presentation of serious thought, such as the pulpit, the press, and the novel, have decreased the significance of the drama as a factor in the life of the community. For these reasons the drama has ceased to be, what it was in the Elizabethan era, the chosen vehicle of the highest intellects for the conveyance of thought to their contemporaries.

The second tendency is a gradual decrease of the importance of the element of 'action' in poetry, strictly so called—that is, creative literature in verse. When 'thought' became dominant over 'form,' and, as the critics recognised, the chief merit of poetry came to be its 'interpretative power,' the presentation of human action tended to become of less importance ; and from the end of the last century onwards poetry has devoted itself in an increasing degree to recording phases of human consciousness, and discovering the spiritual principles which underlie the material phenomena of nature. No one who has watched the motives of modern poetry in England, and in Germany and France, and who has compared these motives with the motives of the classical and Elizabethan poets, can have failed to notice that 'action' has ceased to possess the exceptional importance which it once possessed. Such an importance as it held in the Greek theory of poetry, for example, the theory which inspired the words which Matthew Arnold writes in his 'Irish Essays' : 'What are the eternal objects of poetry among all nations and at all times ? They are actions, human actions, possessing an inherent interest in themselves, and which are to be communicated in an interesting manner by the art of the poet.'

The novel, then, has gathered importance in two respects. It has taken the place of the drama as the chief vehicle for conveying serious thoughts by imagined pictures of life ; and its special capacity for the portrayal of contemporary human action has been emphasised by the fact that poetry in verse has manifested an increasing tendency to become reflective rather than dramatic.

Moreover, as a species of literature, the novel is capable of combining in itself the creations of poetry with the details of history and the generalised experience of philosophy, in a manner unattempted by any previous effort of human genius. Immature as yet and partially developed, it already exercises a portentous control over the mind of the century. Appealing primarily to the youth of the nation, it yet retains its attractiveness for octogenarian statesmen. If, like Aaron's rod, the novel becomes a living thing, who can doubt but that it will swallow up the wands of the magicians ?

The prevalence of the novel has produced a feeling of disquietude in the literary conscience of the age. The recognised guardians of this conscience have expressed alarm and even abhorrence, and there has been much prophesying of evil. But in spite of this general condemnation, when we meet with these critics giving an opinion about a particular novel, we are astonished to find them pronouncing a verdict in the opposite sense. We find Amiel, of whom Matthew Arnold writes that criticism was his true vocation, instantly recognising the message of *Lothair*, and laying the book down with the remark, ' It is exactly my own idea.' We find Emerson telling us in almost one and the same breath that the novel ' has not yet found a tongue,' and that the

popularity of *Jane Eyre* is due to the fact that it has
answered a ' central question.' It is true that he qualifies
this unconscious admission by adding ' in some sort,' but his
subsequent remarks show that he attaches importance to
the answer notwithstanding its limitations. And Matthew
Arnold himself, in his review of Tolstoi's *Anna Karénine*,
doubts whether the author has added much by his subsequent prose works to the religious teaching embodied
in the novel. While as to the pleasure which he enjoyed
in the perusal of it, this is so great that he frankly expresses his regret that Count Tolstoï had (temporarily)
abandoned the career of an artist in prose.

In fact it almost seems as if the general distrust and
disregard of the novel, manifested by the high-priests
and guardians of literature, was really due to a feeling of
prejudice. For while they condemn the novel as a
vehicle of thought, they often express unrestrained
admiration for the message it conveys. We feel in-
clined to exclaim, *tantæne animis cælestibus iræ ?* and
when we cast about for an explanation, or at least an
excuse, for so strange an attitude of mind, we are driven
to suppose that the critics have hitherto regarded the
novel as an intruder in the circle of the arts, and have
not yet cared to make themselves fully acquainted with
the credentials it bears, and the qualities and resources of
which it is possessed. That the general public of novel
readers have felt a desire to have their minds set at rest,
or at any rate to have the witchery of the thing explained, is shown by the fact that the makers of novels
have themselves come forward to explain and justify
their art.

Among English novelists Mr. George Meredith has

alone given an account of fiction which approaches a
definite theory. As Mr. Meredith has been deservedly
styled the 'laureate' of fiction, it will not (before considering this important contribution to the science of
criticism) be out of place to point out one element in
his success, which is closely connected with the literary
medium which he has adopted for the presentation of
his thought. If we except Shakespeare, no writer has
developed the capacity of prose to an equal extent. By
this I mean that Mr. Meredith understands the power
and use of words; that he realises that words unfettered
by metre are a more sensitive, a more powerful, and
a more universal instrument for reaching the imagination
than words in metre ; that prose and not verse is
destined to be the supreme vehicle for the expression
of human ideas. His sentences are, therefore, com-
pacted with the same delicacy as compositions in metre,
but the care which in verse is expended on musical
cadence is here dedicated to exactness of expression and
fulness of meaning. The aspect of the thought of the
age which Mr. Meredith especially embodies in his
prose writings is its widened psychological insight, and
in prose fiction he finds the fittest literary instrument
for the more effective representation of life which the
mental advance of the present century has rendered
possible. For him, then, 'the fiction which is the summary
of actual life, the within and without of us, is, prose or
verse, plodding or soaring, philosophy's elect handmaiden.'
And so he seeks in the novel to give 'a flavour of the
modern day,' which revives the flavour of Shakespeare.

The account to which I have alluded—and from
which I have taken the phrases quoted above—is found

in the first chapter of *Diana of the Crossways*. Here
Mr. Meredith gives us his view of the present condition
of fiction, and his opinion of the direction in which it
must develop—a direction which, we may presume, his
own work is intended to pursue. Fiction is, as now
named by our graver seniors, 'The pastime of idiots, a
method for idiotising the entire population which has
taken to reading ; and which soon discovers that it can
write likewise, that sort of stuff at least.' The day has
come, therefore, when the novelist's art must 'attain its
majority ; ' if not, it is 'doomed to extinction under the
shining multitude of its professors.' The time for the
old ideal, the hero of romance, has gone by. The presentation of the romantically ideal has not been useless ;
on the contrary, it has 'helped to civilise the world ; ' it
has 'led up men from their flint and arrowhead caverns
to intercommunicative daylight ; ' but in this daylight
'intimate acquaintance with a flattering familiar' becomes 'the most dangerous of delusions.'

The redemption of fiction can only be accomplished
by the assistance of philosophy. If the higher conception
of fiction be admitted, the novelist can then be

'veraciously historical, honestly transcriptive. Rose-pink and
dirty drab will alike have passed away. Philosophy is the foe
of both, and their silly cancelling contest, perpetually renewed
in a shuffle of extremes, as it always is where a phantom false-
ness reigns, will no longer baffle the contemplation of natural
flesh, smother no longer the soul issuing out of our incessant
strife. Philosophy bids us see that we are not so pretty as rose-
pink, not so repulsive as dirty drab ; and that, instead of ever-
lastingly shifting those barren aspects, the sight of ourselves is
wholesome, bearable, fructifying, finally a delight.'

From the same point of view he writes that fiction without philosophy 'is a picture of figures modelled on no skeleton-anatomy,' but, with philosophy in aid, it 'blooms, and is humanly shapely.'

Further, by means of philosophy, the novelist can 'minister to growth.' He can provide 'brainstuff' for his readers, and this brainstuff is, in the case of fiction, 'internal history,' or psychological analysis, and 'to suppose it dull is the profoundest of errors.'

Philosophy then enables the novelist to perfect his figures, but from what source does he derive the rough materials for his plots and persons ? How is he to follow the advice which is given 'to follow the diarist, and transcribe from knowledge ? ' A hint of the source and method is given in the novel itself. After Diana, the wayward heroine, has commenced her literary career, we read that she has taken a gentleman of her acquaintance—Percy Dacier—for the model of the hero in her novel entitled *A Minister of State*. But her friend, Emma Dunstane, is assured by her that 'her perusal of the model was an artist's—free, open, and not discoloured by the personal tincture.' And in conversation with Dacier himself, she says in reply to his question, 'May I presume on what is currently reported ? '—'Parts, parts ; a bit here, a bit there. Authors find their models where they can, and generally hit on the nearest.

The artistic principle of word-painting in the presentation of character is stated in the sentence, to which reference has been already made : [1] 'The art of the pen is to rouse the inward vision . . . because our flying minds cannot contain a protracted description. . . .

[1] Chapter vi. p. 109.

The Shakespearian, the Dantesque [pictures], are in a
line, two at most.'

In a similar sense Sir Walter Besant writes, after
describing the almost unconscious growth of characters
in the novelist's mind :

'That is the highest art which carries the reader along and
makes him see, without being told, the changing expressions,
the gestures of the speakers, and hear the varying tones of their
voices. . . . The only writer who can do this is he who makes
his characters intelligible from the very outset, causes them to
stand before the reader in clear outline, and then with every
additional line brings out the figure, fills up the face, and makes
his creations grow from the simple outline more and more to the
perfect and rounded figure.'

To this theoretic statement we may add the actual
record of 'George Eliot's' experience, given in her Diary
and Correspondence. [1]

Of *Adam Bede* she says :

'There is not a single portrait in the book, nor will there be
in any future book of mine. There are portraits in the *Clerical
Scenes ;* but that was my first bit of art, and my hand was
not well in. I did not know so well how to manipulate my
materials.'

Again she writes in correcting a mistake :

'I do wish much to see more of human life; how can one
see enough in the short years one has to stay in the world ?
But I meant that at present my mind works with the most
freedom and the keenest sense of poetry in my remotest past,
and there are many strata to be worked through before I can
begin to use *artistically* any material I may gather in the
present.'

[1] *George Eliot's Life*, W. J. Cross.

In other words, she kept closely to the Aristotelian canon of presenting types, not individuals; the joint productions of actual experience and mental processes. Her best writing, she considered, was that produced in moments when she was taken out of herself, and possessed, as it were, by the persons of her creation.

'Particularly,' says her biographer, 'she dwelt on this in regard to the scene in *Middlemarch* between Dorothea and Rosamund, saying that, though she always knew that they had sooner or later to come together, she kept the idea resolutely out of her mind until Dorothea was in Rosamund's drawing-room. Then, abandoning herself to the inspiration of the moment, she wrote the whole scene exactly as it stands, without alteration or erasure, in an intense state of excitement and agitation, feeling herself entirely possessed by the feelings of the two women.'

And the final scene in the *Mill on the Floss* was written in the same white heat.

But apart from using philosophy to provide a 'skeleton-anatomy' for his characters, Mr. Meredith teaches its truths by a method which, designedly or not, reproduces in the novel the part played by the chorus in the Greek tragedy. It consists in the introduction of a number of biting sentences, which generally illustrate some cardinal point in the plot. The two novels in which these sentences are most prominent are *Richard Feverel* and *Diana of the Crossways*. In the former we get as a comment on the story of Austin Wentworth, and the harsh judgment of the world on him: *The compensation for injustice is, that in that dark ordeal we gather the worthiest around us.* And in counsel to his son, Sir Austin Feverel quotes from *The Pilgrim's Scrip*, the source to which these philosophic aphorisms are referred in the novel in question : *Who rises from prayer a better man, his prayer is answered.* In *Diana of the Crossways* the sayings purport to be the remarks of the heroine preserved in *The Leaves from the Diary of Henry Wilmers.* Of romance Mrs. Warwick says : *The young who avoid that region escape the title of fool at the cost of a celestial crown.* And the lesson of her life is summarised in the sentence : *There is nothing the body suffers that the soul may not profit by.*

Another writer of fiction,[1] in a recent essay, has called the novel 'a pocket-theatre.' The expression has the merit of picturesqueness, and it is valuable as pointing directly to the significant consideration that the modern novel is in a certain sense the descendant of the Greek tragedy and the Elizabethan play : that, in point of fact, it is the novel and not the theatre on which has devolved the task of furnishing that ideal presentation of life which, directly springing from the primitive instinct of imitation, has never ceased to form a chief source of delight and instruction to civilised man. But apart from the external differences of form and method, which are too apparent to need enumeration, the scope and character of the ideal representation of life, at which tragedy, play, and novel alike aim, has undergone a change. The working of the modern democratic spirit, while it tends to weaken institutions by lessening the distinctions of rank and nationality, heightens and develops individual life ; and whereas the Greeks and the Elizabethan Englishmen desired to contemplate the central ideas of religion and humanity chiefly as embodied in their national life and

[1] Mr. Marion Crawford.

history, it is the most salient features in the career of an individual that now command our keenest attention. The fact that the point of view from which life is regarded has changed is one reason, but it is not the sole reason, for the change in the vehicle by which the picture of life is presented. Life itself has changed. It has changed not merely in those external aspects of which our railways and steamships, our telegraph wires and our newspapers, are the outward and visible sign, but the horizon of each individual mind has been extended and enlarged. Consider the difference between the sensations which an average Greek of the age of Pericles, or an Elizabethan Englishman, could compass in a given period of time, and those which we experience to-day in point of number, variety, and intensity. Compare the budget of a ' well-girt messenger ' or an express trireme, with the columns of news which we read in a daily newspaper. Or the home-brewed ale, the beef and bread that formed the staple of Elizabethan diet, with the cosmopolitan display, in which no limits of climate or season are recognised, which characterises our modern tables. And the picture of life which the artist nature is impelled to give forth must be correspondingly full and complete, if mankind is still to feel pleasure in beholding it. The theatre, with the rigorous limitations essential to dramatic art, could not, however perfectly its resources were marshalled and arranged, present to the mind such a picture as can alone reflect the intricate and varied spectacle which the life of man has now become.

And there is another reason why the drama is insufficient to contain the fulness of nineteenth-century life. Part of the pictures of life which we want to see cannot be represented on the stage at all. Thought, with all the shades and refinements of motive which characterise the modern mind, possesses a predominant attractiveness at the present time. But thought cannot be represented on the stage except in a soliloquy or an aside. How could the stage afford us such a picture of a human mind as that which 'George Eliot' gives us, when she describes Arthur Donnithorne's visit to Mr. Irwine? Or of the workings of a woman's reason, such as Mr. Meredith gives us in that chapter in which he describes the feelings of Diana, when, in her retirement at the Crossways, she at length decides to face 'a woman's brutallest tussle with the world'? And if it be objected that such lengthy descriptions are inartistic; that, in the words of Mr. Meredith himself, 'The art of the pen is to rouse the inward vision instead of labouring with a drop-scene brush,' I reply, 'True; but whether the pen may be said to labour or not depends upon the extent of the scenery it has to paint.' Such descriptions as have been instanced do not aim at producing a single vision, but a kaleidoscopic series of visions. In fact the objection serves to emphasise the point advanced; for it shows that the working of the mind, which is now recognised by the dramatic artist as suitable for representation, is a new field. The representation of this mental phenomena, in the full and complete form which is attempted by the novel, is rendered at once possible and necessary by the increased psychological knowledge of the age in which we live.

It would be interesting to work out the comparison in its completeness, and show how tragedy, play, and novel differ in their accidental, but agree in their essential qualities, as vehicles for the delineation of contemporary life. How the same principles govern the poetic element of creation appearing in plot and character ; how the narrative speeches recited by the ἄγγελος in the tragedy, and the stage scenery, find their counterparts in the descriptions of the novel ; how the novelist has his lyric moments as well as the dramatist, and, in spite of the wide intervals which separate Greek from modern life, we can find a central thought in which Sophocles's ' Ode to Love,' and ' George Eliot's ' reflection on the feelings of Seth Bede, the Methodist carpenter, agree. Sophocles tells us of the external action of passion :

> Ἔρως, ἀνίκατε μάχαν.
> Ἔρως, ὃς ἐν κτήμασι πίπτεις,
> ὃς ἐν μαλακαῖς παρειαῖς
> νεάνιδος ἐννυχεύεις,
> φοιτᾷς δ' ὑπερπόντιος ἔν τ' ἀγρονόμοις αὐλαῖς·
> καὶ σ' οὔτ' ἀθανάτων φύξιμος οὐδεὶς
> οὔθ ἀμερίων ἐπ' ἀνθρώπων, ὁ δ' ἔχων μέμηνεν.[1]

' George Eliot,' of its transforming grace :

' Our caresses, our tender words, our still rapture under the influence of autumn sunsets, or pillared vistas, or calm majestic statues, or Beethoven symphonies, all bring with them the consciousness that they are mere waves and ripples in an unfathomable ocean of love and beauty ; our emotion in its keenest

---

[1] Love, unconquered in battle,
Love, spoiler of men,
That makest thy couch on the maiden's soft cheeks,
That walkest on the sea and dwellest in the wilds ;
Of the immortals none can escape thee,
Of short-lived mortals, none ;
He that hath thee is straightway mad.

Antigone, 781–790.

moment passes from expression into silence, our love at its highest flood rushes beyond the object, and loses itself in the sense of divine mystery.'

Or, we might compare the defiant lines with which Medea concludes the soliloquy in which she determines to carry out her scheme of vengeance :

> ἐπίστασαι δέ· πρὸς δὲ καὶ πεφύκαμεν
> γυναῖκες, ἐς μὲν ἔσθλ' ἀμηχανώταται
> κακῶν δὲ πάντων τέκτονες σοφώταται—[1]

with the epigrammatic sentence with which Mr. Meredith starts Sir Austin Feverel on that educational experiment which ended so disastrously : 'I expect that woman will be the last thing civilised by man.'

Or again, we might turn to Shakespeare, and, while rendering homage to the infinite perfection of his method, yet notice those omissions, inherent in the finest drama, which the humblest novel would perforce avoid. Think how a novelist would revel in telling us how Celia managed to escape with Rosalind from her father's palace. Instead of telling us, as Shakespeare does, that

> ' The ladies, her attendants of her chamber,
> Saw her abed, and in the morning early
> They found the bed untreasured of their mistress,'

the whole action might have turned upon the missing of a train, or the loss of a key. Certainly we should expect to be told a good deal more about Oliver, before we were prepared to believe in that sudden 'conversion'

---

[1] It is, besides, a priv'lege of our sex,
  To be for good most helpless, in all bad,
  Cunning beyond dispute.

Medea, 406–8.

which made him the man to woo Celia in the swift Elizabethan fashion of which Rosalind tells Orlando : 'Your brother and my sister no sooner met but they looked, no sooner looked but they loved, no sooner loved but they sighed, no sooner sighed but they asked one another the reason, no sooner knew the reason but they sought the remedy.'

Considerations such as these bring us face to face with the cardinal point in the discussion of the claims of the novel. For the rendering of its ideal representation of life the novel relies solely on the power of language. As a form of literature it embodies a new conception of poetry analogous to that new conception of art foreshadowed in Emerson's essay—a conception which includes the railroad and the mill, the chemist's retort and the galvanic battery, among the things intended for its divine uses.[1] Is this new form of poetry one in which artistic excellence must be secondary to scientific exactness ? Is this new picture of life to lack that paramount element of mind, idealisation, which is the essential characteristic of a work of art ? In a word, are we having in the novel photographs of life instead of pictures ?

These questions throw us back upon the first principles of art. But first we may notice that a good photograph has a worth and usefulness of its own. It is not a portrait, for it lacks the element of mind. It gives us the expression of a moment and not a synthesis of expressions ; it reproduces all the accessory details—not just so much as the artist would select. But it tells us what a person, or a place, is like. And such novels as contain a record of actual experience, being in fact copies of nature

---

[1] *Essay on Art*, First Series.

faithfully drawn, are useful, if only we do not mistake them for works of art. But to return. What is the end of art? To interpret life and nature. All are agreed in that. *L'expression est la loi suprème de l'art*, says Cousin. And Arnold, the grand power of poetry is its 'interpretative power.' And Mr. Ruskin, when he is trying to find a test of excellence in art so wide that it will include all its manifestations and forms, concludes that 'the art is greatest which conveys to the spectator, by any means whatsoever, the greatest number of the greatest ideas.' But how are these ideas to be conveyed? how is this interpretation to be accomplished? Clearly by the methods of the several arts which, differing among themselves, agree in this, that they all alike aim at affecting the imagination. Works of art are produced, Cousin writes, because man desires to see again the beauty which has delighted him in nature or in real life. But he does not desire to see this in the same form; if he did he must go back to nature and real life. He desires to see it in the form in which the imagination represents it.

For this work of interpreting nature by playing upon the imagination, the novel in its own sphere—that of presenting an ideal representation of contemporary life—is in no sense deficient. It relies solely on the power of words, claiming neither the music of verse nor the actuality of the drama, but what the representation has lost in these respects it has gained in freedom and completeness. This sole instrument, language, of which the novel, more than any other form of creative literature, has an absolute command, is the most powerful of all the instruments which the arts employ to affect the imagination. *Can all the trappings or equipage of a king or hero give Brutus half that pomp and majesty which he receives from a few lines in Shakespeare ?* [1]

Nor is it unable to speak with that distinctive accent which arises from the ' high seriousness of absolute sincerity.' 'George Eliot' uses it at times in speaking of Dorothea, of Hetty Sorrel, and of Maggie Tulliver. It is surely with this accent that she says of Romola :

' No radiant angel came across the gloom with a clear message for her. In those times, as now, there were human beings who never saw angels or heard perfectly clear messages. Such truth as came to them was brought confusedly in the voices and deeds of men not at all like the seraphs of unfailing wing and piercing vision—men who believed falsities as well as truths, and did the wrong as well as the right. The helping hands stretched out to them were the hands of men who stumbled and often saw dimly, so that these beings unvisited by angels had no other choice than to grasp that stumbling guidance along the path of reliance and action, which is the path of life, or else to pause in loneliness and disbelief, which is no path, but the arrest of inaction and death.'

[1] Addison.

CHAPTER XII

In the preceding chapters an attempt has been made to set out the rules which govern the processes of artistic production, as they have been formulated by the several writers whose opinions have been cited. These rules differ only from observed uniformities in so far as they have been connected by each writer with some characteristic of the human mind. But since the human mind—that is, the sum total of man's conscious knowledge—changes with the development of the race, the rules of any one writer, of any one age, even when thus fortified, have only a partial and limited validity. When, however, we find a practical agreement on certain points between writers widely separated by intervals of time and circumstance, we are led to the conclusion that there are certain principles underlying these rules which have a permanent validity.

To exhibit this agreement, and these principles, has been one chief object of the analyses which have been submitted to the reader.

Broadly stated, the authority of the critic depends upon the fact of this agreement; and in order to maintain his authority he must do two things: he must distinguish between the rules which are partial, and the principles which are permanent ; and he must confine himself to an application of the latter.

This is the goal towards which criticism has advanced ; towards which it is still steadily advancing. Its development exhibits a gradual limitation of the scope of its rules, and a gradual extension of the scope of its principles. In other words, the critic shows an increased and increasing capacity to discern what is amenable to his authority, and to confine himself to an examination of this element in the products of the special art which is the subject of his researches.

With Plato the critic is the legislator, who declares with the authority of the State both the subjects and the methods of the arts. With Aristotle he is the representative of Homer and Sophocles, who would make all epics Homeric, and all plays Sophoclean. Modern criticism commenced from this point. The seventeenth-century critic was the exponent of the *Poetics*, and even Addison began with the notion that *Paradise Lost* could somehow be measured by Aristotle's canons. But Addison, as we know, emerged from this stage, and discovered a principle of poetic appeal which enabled him and all subsequent critics to transcend mere formal considerations, by substituting the 'power to effect the imagination' for the test of symmetry. In so doing he emphasised the fact that the achievement itself, and not the means employed to secure that achievement, ought to be the first object of a critic's consideration. If Lessing returned to the consideration of processes rather than results, and devoted himself to distinguishing the respective methods and resources of the contrasting arts of the eye and ear, he was nevertheless guided in his researches by the realisation of this same truth—that the appeal of the arts was in all cases not to the senses, but to the imagination through the senses. Similarly Cousin, starting with the same truth expressed in terms of philosophy—that it is the ideal and not the real which is the object of artistic presentation—traces in broad outline the mental processes which accompany and distinguish artistic activities, and indicates the place which the sense of beauty holds as part of the intellectual and moral faculties of man.

The result of this change of the point of view is to be seen in the practice of contemporary critics. An enlightened criticism no longer aims at directing the artist by formulating rules which, if they were valid, would only tend to obliterate the distinction between the fine and the mechanical arts. It allows him to work by whatever methods he may choose ; and it is content to estimate his merit, not by reference to his method, but by reference to his achievement as measured by principles of universal validity. In this way it avoids the danger of pronouncing an opinion on what is variable, and applies itself to what is permanent.

The power of the artist is, as we say, a gift : *poeta nascitur*, *non fit*. To attempt to formulate a set of rules, or to decide the value of artistic products by reference to these rules, is to forget this elementary principle ; and from this mistake, made so persistently and continuously, criticism is now at length emerging. It is unnecessary to go over the ground which has been traversed by Wordsworth in his ' Essay supplementary to the Preface ' of his edition of 1815, and more recently by Mr. Dowden.[1] Criticism has failed because it has under-

[1] ' Interpretation of Literature,' *Contemporary Review*, 1886.

taken—or rather its self-ordained representatives, the critics of the journals, have undertaken, on its behalf, a task beyond their powers. 'If there be one conclusion more forcibly pressed upon us than another,' says Wordsworth,

'by the review which has been given of the fortunes and fate of poetical works, it is this: that every author, as far as he is great and at the same time *original*, has had the task of creating the taste by which he is to be enjoyed; so has it been, so will it continue to be. . . . The predecessors of an original genius of a high order will have smoothed the way for all that he has in common with them; and much he will have in common; but, for what is peculiarly his own, he will be called upon to clear and often to shape his own road; he will be in the condition of Hannibal among the Alps.'

The critics have gone astray in the past, because in applying rules they have failed to make allowance in their estimates for this unknown quantity. What is original is *ex hypothesi* something for which known rules, and existing works, provide no exact standards of measurement or comparison.

Criticism, then, has reached the stage in which it is beginning to distinguish between principles and rules. It places the technical element, which is covered by these rules, entirely on one side, or if it approaches that element, it does so with a full consciousness of the partial validity of the rules which it applies. But it investigates with increased energy and insight the permanent element of thought, the ideal element, which is produced in accordance with certain principles which have become part of the life of man, and which are capable of being universally recognised as such.

Let me try to make my meaning plain by an example. When Addison adopts the system of seventeenth-century criticism and writes : ' I have now considered Milton's *Paradise Lost* under the four great heads of the Fable, the Characters, the Sentiments, and the Language, and have shown that he excels in general under each of these heads '—he is pronouncing a judgment which has only a limited validity. It is valid only for persons who are conversant with Aristotle's canons, and it is valid only so long as these canons are recognised as the supreme test of poetic excellence.   On the other hand, when Matthew Arnold decides that Milton stands among the poets of the highest class, because his work displays the ' high seriousness of absolute sincerity,' he is deciding the value of his poetry by virtue of a quality which is capable of immediate and universal recognition : and the value of the verdict consists in the fact that its truth or falsity can be ascertained not merely by a limited class of persons, but by all persons of ordinary intelligence. Again, the same thing happens when Mr. Swinburne brushes away the arguments founded upon Byron's technical defects, his want of constructive ability, his ' trailing relatives,' and what not, and answers the question ' whether Byron is or is not a great poet,' by pointing to one quality, ' the splendid and imperishable excellence of sincerity and strength.'

Nevertheless, in approaching this permanent element in literature, critics are still divided into two opposing camps.   Although the recognition of the commanding part played by the imagination in literature has largely modified the value of the test of symmetry as a means of estimating literary merit, yet the dual basis of art still causes individual critics to apply mainly, or exclusively, one of the two central tests, where both should be applied in conjunction. These two tests are, of course, the Platonic test of truth, or harmony with the general sense of mankind, and the Aristotelian test of symmetry, or recognition of the principle of external beauty.

A brief consideration will serve to show that these two tests, which have been so often separated for purposes of criticism, are really to be referred to one and the same standard of authority : in other words that 'technical excellence' and 'ability to please mankind' are one and the same thing.

The process by which a masterpiece becomes a masterpiece is this. The community recognise the merit of the artist's work ; the critics analyse it ; and they apply the result of their analysis to the examination of subsequent productions.

Thus the rules of any art are the summary of what has been observed in the works of the masters in that art. But these works have acquired their pre-eminence not by selection of the critics, but by appreciation of the general mass of the men among whom they were produced. What the critics do is at most to define and explain, to register in fact, preferences already expressed. Just as laws express the sense of the community as manifested in custom, so the rules of art express the public recognition of the skill of the artists as manifested in the acceptance of their works.

If this, then, be a true account of the process by which we arrive at a body of rules in any particular art—if, that is to say, the critics merely record the practice of the masters, and the practice of the masters is determined by the appreciation of the general mass of their fellow-men—then it follows that the merit of a work of art is judged by one single standard—the appreciation of mankind. It is the appreciation of mankind that has determined the practice of the masters in the past ; it is this that determines the practice of the masters in the present, and that will determine it in the future.

And if this reasoning be correct, this important conclusion follows. In the appreciation of mankind the body of thought which, under the name of morality, expresses the experience of the race in general, and of the community in particular, must always be a commanding element. Morality, therefore, in this sense, cannot be separated from artistic excellence ; it is part of the human consciousness which is affected favourably or unfavourably ; which appreciates and assimilates, and by so doing determines what is of permanent value among the various productions of the arts.

The formal criticism, which was applied by the French critics in the seventeenth century was based upon the mistaken belief that the work of the artist could be dissociated from the general sense of mankind and the progress of humanity. Formal criticism of this extreme type is dead ; but the error upon which it was based survives in the doctrine of ' Art for Art's sake.'

The contention of this school of criticism is stated by Mr. Swinburne. Assuming that the critic has a complete knowledge of the art in question, he writes : ' No work of art has any worth or life in it that is not done on the absolute terms of art, that is not, before all things and above all things, a work of positive excellence, as judged

by the laws of the special art to whose laws it is amenable.' In the case of poetry, this positive excellence is
indicated by the presence of an 'ardent harmony.'

'In all great poets there must be an ardent harmony, a heat
of spiritual life, guiding without restraining the bodily grace of
motion, which shall give charm and power to their least work,
sweetness which cannot be weak, and force that will not be
rough. There must be an instinct and resolution of excellence
which will allow of no shortcoming or malformation of thought
or word; there must be also so natural a sense of right as to
make such a deformity or defect impossible, and leave upon the
work done no trace of any effort to avoid or achieve.'

And therefore,

'the worth of a poem has properly nothing to do with its moral
meaning or design; the praise of a Cæsar as sung by a Virgil,
of a Stuart as sung by a Dryden, is preferable to the most
magnanimous invective against tyranny, which love of country
and of liberty could wring from a Bavius or a Settle.'[1]

'Has properly nothing to do . . . ,' that is to say,
if the critic confines himself to technical excellence.
But apart from the difficulty of finding a critic who has
a greater knowledge of the rules of the special art than
the artist himself, a judgment pronounced on these terms
would be valueless, for it would omit to take account of
the one quality the presence of which is essential to
secure the favourable verdict of mankind—the quality
of giving pleasure. What Wordsworth has written of
poetry is applicable to all the fine arts. There is a limit
beyond which the artist must not exercise his technical
power. Speaking of the higher validity of poetic truth
as compared with that of history or biography, he says:[2]

[1] *Essays and Studies.*
[2] Observations prefixed to the second edition of *Lyrical Ballads.*

'The poet writes under one restriction only, namely, that of the necessity of giving immediate pleasure to a human being possessed of that information which may be expected from him, not as a lawyer, a physician, a mariner, an astronomer, or a natural philosopher, but as a man. Except this one restriction, there is no object standing between the poet and the image of things ; between this and the biographer and historian there are a thousand.'

Poet, painter, sculptor—all alike work subject to the one and identical restriction : if they would produce something of permanent value as a work of art—some gift which mankind will accept—they must satisfy the general sense of mankind. This, then, is the tribunal which gives the final verdict of success or failure.

It is from a due appreciation of this truth, and a due acknowledgment of this restriction, that Mr. Ruskin makes morality—that is, harmony with the general sense of mankind in its most clear and permanent manifestation—at once the foundation of the artist's power and the test of the merit of his work. Insisting upon this restriction, he writes,[1] in a sense precisely opposite to that of Mr. Swinburne :

'All right human song is, similarly, the finished expression, by art, of the joy or grief of noble persons, for right causes. And accurately in proportion to the rightness of the cause, and purity of the emotion, is the possibility of the fine art. . . . And with absolute precision, from highest to lowest, the fineness of the possible art is an index of the moral purity and majesty of the emotion it expresses. . . . And that is so in all the arts ; so that with mathematical precision, subject to no error or exception, the art of a nation, so far as it exists, is an exponent of its ethical state.'

[1] *Lectures on Art*, iii. § 67.

And again, when he is seeking for 'a definition of Art wide enough to include all its varieties of aim,' he writes :

'I do not say, therefore, that the art is greatest which gives most pleasure, because perhaps there is some art whose end is to teach and not to please.   I do not say that the art is greatest which teaches us most, because perhaps there is some art whose end is to please and not to teach.   I do not say that the art is greatest which imitates best, because perhaps there is some art whose end is to create and not to imitate.   But I say that the art is greatest which conveys to the spectator, by any means whatsoever, the greatest number of the greatest ideas ; and I call an idea great in proportion as it is received by a higher faculty of the mind, and as it more fully occupies, and in occupying, exercises and exalts, the faculty by which it is received.   If this, then, be the definition of great art, that of a great artist naturally follows.   He is the greatest artist who has embodied, in the sum of his works, the greatest number of the greatest ideas.' [1]

And so Mr. Ruskin's criticism is an attempt to decide the value of the products of the arts purely by reference to this test—the test of harmony with the sense of mankind as contained in the moral decisions of a given society. 'In these books of mine,' he says, 'their distinctive character as Essays on Art is their bringing everything to a root in human passion or human hope.' [2]

The implied antithesis between artistic excellence and morality, which is contained in the theory of 'Art for Art's sake,' disappears, therefore, when the nature of the authority which pronounces judgment upon works of art is analysed.   And, in fact, the surest assistance which

[1] *Modern Painters*, I. part 1, section 1, chapter ii. § 9.
[2] Ib. V. part 9, section 1, § 7.

the critic receives in the task of gauging the value of
new work prior to the verdict of posterity, is that which
he derives from an examination of the highest previous
achievements in the branch of art to which this new
work belongs. In other words, he estimates the pros-
pects which the new work has of satisfying mankind,
by comparing it with work upon which the same tribunal
has already pronounced a favourable verdict.

Comparison with the masterpieces underlies all these
judgments tentatively pronounced by the critic. Literary
taste, says Addison,[1] is the faculty 'which discerns the
beauties of an author with pleasure and the imperfections
with dislike. If a man would know whether he is possessed of this faculty, I would have him read over the
celebrated works of antiquity, which have stood the test
of so many different ages and countries . . .' And
Arnold gives the same advice in his essay on the *Study
of Poetry*. Similarly art criticism, strictly so called,
is an examination of the works of great artists, and a
declaration of the excellences so revealed ; or, if it
becomes constructive, it is an attempt to reduce the
practice of the artists to a system. But in all these
cases the critic does not pronounce the verdict which
gives such work its value ; he merely interprets or formulates a judgment previously expressed by the general
sense of mankind. In the case of contemporary work
he attempts to anticipate this verdict, by comparing the
new work with old work which has satisfied the general
sense of mankind.

Whereas, however, the critic applies this test of
harmony with the general sense of mankind only in-

[1] *Spectator*, 409.

directly, that is to say, through his knowledge of works which have already satisfied it, the artist applies the test directly in the practice of his art. And for this reason the most humble artist feels that, in trying to satisfy the general sense of mankind, he is obeying an authority of higher validity than the most accomplished critic.

> ' Five acts to make a play.
> And why not fifteen ? why not ten ? or seven ?
> What matter for the number of the leaves,
> Supposing the tree lives and grows ? exact
> The literal unities of time and place,
> When 't is the essence of passion to ignore
> Both time and place ? Absurd. Keep up the fire,
> And leave the generous flames to shape themselves.
>
> .   .   .   .   .
>
> And whosoever writes good poetry,
> Looks just to art. He does not write for you
> Or me—for London or for Edinborough ;
> He will not suffer the best critic known
> To step into his sunshine of free thought
> And self-absorbed conception, and exact
> An inch-long swerving of the holy lines.
> If virtue done for popularity
> Defiles like vice, can art, for praise or hire,
> Still keep its splendour and remain pure art ?
> Eschew such serfdom. What the poet writes,
> He writes : mankind accepts it if it suits,
> And that's success : if not, the poem's passed
> From hand to hand, and yet from hand to hand
> Until the unborn snatch it, crying out
> In pity on their fathers' being so dull,
> And that's success too.' [1]

[1] *Aurora Leigh*, Book V.

I find in these lines of Elizabeth Barrett Browning a true statement of the actual relationship of the artist both to the critic and to the general mass of mankind. And, as I have already pointed out, criticism exhibits an increasing tendency to recognise these limits, and to confine itself to the interpretation of the ideal element in literature and art.

Critical writers both in England and on the Continent have come to recognise that the critic's business is less with the poet and the artist, than with the reader and the spectator. Such writers do not try to tell the poet how to compose, or the painter how to paint ; they rather teach us how to admire. This criticism possesses a real and appreciable value. It distributes a knowledge of those characteristics of the best work in the several arts which can be conveyed by the medium of language. It is both honest and effective. It treats of what can be treated of by literature—the idea ; and it conveys a kind of knowledge in which the layman is naturally most deficient. The eye is unconsciously trained to an appreciation of form and colour by the observation of objects in the ordinary business of life. It is not difficult to trace the resemblance between works of art and the originals which they imitate ; nor do the characters of the poet differ in their external attributes from the men and women of every-day life. But the ideas, the moral beauty embodied in these forms of physical beauty (or in the symbols which represent these forms), have no external counterparts, and require, therefore, to be explained and interpreted. It is this useful office which contemporary criticism especially performs ; and a perception of the ideal aspects of poetry and the arts has become as much a characteristic of modern critical inquiry as scientific exactness is of our study of nature and of man.

And so in the writings of successive critics we have a record of the passage from unconscious to conscious appreciation of beauty in literature and in works of art.

For the work of criticism has been to analyse, to formulate, and finally to reduce to terms of common thought effects produced from the first birth of art, but effects which have increased in force and vividness with the development of the intellectual and moral faculties of man.

I. INDEX OF AUTHORS QUOTED

A

237

NOTE.—The above contains only the names of authors directly cited. The names of other authors to whom reference is made are included in the Subject Index.

II. INDEX OF SUBJECTS

A

N

O

P

THE END